Lisbon

Also by Malcolm Jack

The Social and Political Thought of Bernard Mandeville
Corruption and Progress: The Eighteenth-Century Debate
William Beckford: An English Fidalgo
Sintra: A Glorious Eden
The Turkish Embassy Letters of Lady Mary Wortley Montagu
 (ed.)
Vathek and Other Stories: A William Beckford Reader (ed.)
The Episodes of Vathek (ed.)

Lisbon

City of the Sea

A History

MALCOLM JACK

I.B. TAURIS

LONDON · NEW YORK

Published in 2007 by I.B.Tauris & Co. Ltd
6 Salem Rd, London W2 4BU
175 Fifth Avenue, New York NY 10010
www.ibtauris.com

Supported by

CALOUSTE
GULBENKIAN
FOUNDATION

In the United States and Canada distributed by Palgrave Macmillan,
a division of St. Martin's Press, 175 Fifth Avenue, New York, NY 10010

ISBN 978 1 84511 403 9

A full CIP record for this book is available from the British Library
A full CIP record for this book is available from the Library of Congress
Library of Congress catalog card: available

Typeset in ITC Bodoni Book by illuminati, Grosmont,
www.illuminatibooks.co.uk
Printed and bound in Great Britain by
TJ International Ltd, Padstow, Cornwall

Contents

List of Illustrations

Dom Fernando de Saxe-Coburg Gotha. Lithograph, *c.* 1850 (Sintra, Municipal Archive).

Antonio Feliciano de Castilho, 1859, in A. Pimentel, *Fotografias de Lisboa*, 1874.

Rua Augusta by Alex Michellis, 1842 (Museu da Cidade, Lisbon).

Alexandre Herculano by Alberto, *c.* 1870, in A. Pimentel, *Fotografias de Lisboa*, 1874.

Between pages 140 and 141

The Lisbon Aqueduct. Engraving by G. Vivien, nineteenth century (Museu da Cidade, Lisbon).

Terreiro do Paço. Painting by D. Stoop, 1662 (Museu da Cidade, Lisbon).

The Tower of Belém. (Photograph by Nuno Antunes, 2006.)

Lisbon Cathedral. (Photograph by Nuno Antunes, 2006.)

View of the Tagus and Bridge of 25 April. (Photograph by Nuno Antunes, 2006.)

Ministry of Justice, Praça do Comércio. (Photograph by Nuno Antunes, 2006.)

View of St George's Castle and Rossio Square. (Photograph by Nuno Antunes, 2006.)

Monument of the Explorers. Cottinelli Telmo, 1960 (Photograph by Nuno Antunes, 2006.).

Marquês de Pombal. Painting by Louis Michael Van Loo, 1766 (Museu da Cidade, Lisbon).

Ruins of St Nicholas Church. Coloured etching by Jacques Philippe Le Bas, 1757. (Museu da Cidade, Lisbon).

Ruins of the Opera House. Coloured etching by Jacques Philippe Le Bas, 1757 (Museu da Cidade, Lisbon).

Marquês de Pombal. Painting, attrib. J. de Salitre, 1770 (Museu da Cidade, Lisbon).

Acknowledgements

This book grew out of another, namely *Sintra: A Glorious Eden*, which was published in 2002, exactly a hundred years after *Historic Macao* appeared in the name of a rather eccentric member of my mother's maternal family.[1] It would not have been possible to write about Sintra without reference to Lisbon, so in the preparation of that work I had already amassed an archive of material on Lisbon itself. Reviewing those papers, it occurred to me that a sister book to *Sintra* would be a good idea, so I gathered more material. I wrote much of the book in faraway Cape Town, where Portuguese connections are not entirely absent. The chapter on the Lisbon earthquake of 1755 first appeared in a different form in a collection of essays especially commissioned to mark the 250th anniversary of the event.[2]

I must thank Liz Friend-Smith of I.B. Tauris, my publisher, for so enthusiastically taking up the project, and the publisher himself for actually producing the book. I once again have had the support of the Gulbenkian Foundation, London, for which I am grateful. Acknowledgements for this book must include mention of Professor João Flor and Dr Pedro Flor, both proud citizens of Lisbon, who have always been enthusiastic supporters of my Lusitanian projections. I must also thank the Gilda Nunes Barata and Rosário Dantas of the Museu da Cidade for her help and the Museum for allowing me to reproduce the images from its extensive and elegantly housed collection. I also thank colleagues at the Sintra Archives for their help in the past, Nuno Antunes for his fine photos, and his assistant Jorge Matreno. Here at home I am grateful to the ever patient Robert Borsje, who also knows Lisbon well and is such a fine geographer. Lisbon has a rich historiography, particularly in Portuguese, so I have also been guided by generations of writers, poets and artists in refining my appreciation of a truly magnificent city.

SPAIN

MINHO
• BRAGA

TRAZ-OS-
MONTES
• VILA REAL

RIO DOURO

PORTO
•
DOURO
LITORAL

BEIRA ALTA
• VISEU
RIO MONDEGO

BEIRA LITORAL

COIMBRA
•

BEIRA
BAIXA
• CASTELO-BRANCO

RIO TEJO

ESTREMADURA

SANTAREM
•
RIO TEJO

RIBATEJO

ALTO
ALENTEJO

• EVORA

SPAIN

LISBON
•

RIO SADO
BEJA
•
RIO GUADIANA

BAIXO
ALENTEJO

OCÉANO
ATLÁNTICO

ALGARVE
FARO
•

Map of Portugal

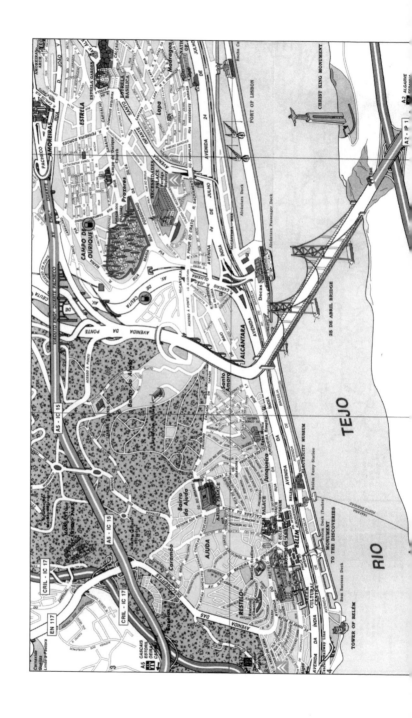

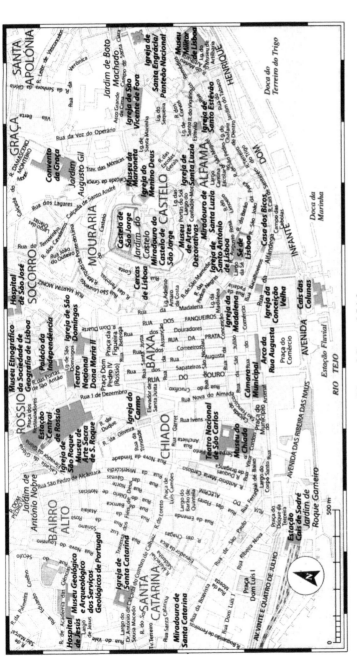

Map of Central Lisbon

To
Carlos Alberto Pacheco Jorge and João António Santos,
who both, in different ways, loved the city

Preface

To write a history of a city is to write about a person as well as a place. When the city is ancient, like Lisbon, its personality will be complex and many-layered. Some aspects of the city's story will be repetitive – over and over again the sea figures in the history of Lisbon – but other features will be ephemeral. The sellers of holy relics no longer throng the religious institutions of the city hawking their dubious wares. They have been replaced by a new breed of streetwise vendors who tout the latest fashions in clothes or in gadgets at bargain prices.

Writing about a person suggests a chronology since each individual has his own personal history, but to understand the personality of the city we need to pursue themes which cross over historical ages. These connecting threads are sometimes communal – the Roman Catholic Church has been established in the city for centuries; foreigners, such as the English, have long played a part in its development. Millions of Lisbon's inhabitants have grown up within view of the river and have earned their living on the waters of it or in industries and commerce connected with the sea. Treating our subject in themes will tempt us to look for influences to explain how this or that came about; historical accounts will shed light on our perspectives.

The character of Lisbon has also been formed by its geography. Like Rome it is founded on seven hills; it is at the estuary of a great navigable river, the Tagus. To the west are vast tracts of the Atlantic bringing an oceanic coolness and dampness to soften the severity of a southern climate. It is exceptionally mild in winter with no snow and little frost. Its hinterland is fertile; its geological make-up is seismic. In 1755 a great earthquake destroyed a large part of the city. To these bare geographical facts can be added a political history that has turned the focus of Portugal more towards the overseas rather than inland towards continental Europe. Its Iberian neighbour, Spain, has often been perceived as a threat to its nationhood, which was established early; for a period of sixty years in the sixteenth century the threat became a reality when Portugal was annexed by the Spanish crown. Real or perceived, the geographical position of Spain has meant that Portugal has been cut off from mainstream Europe. We might say that Lisbon, as a result, has been stretched in one direction toward Brazil and in another, southward, toward the Cape of Good Hope, and from there eastwards to Asia.

Tracing historical themes will involve us in tracing literary and artistic responses to the city as well. Medieval chroniclers had already described details of Lisbon by the time Damião de Góis wrote his celebrated observations in 1554. The city has always appeared to them and those who have followed as a labyrinth: outward voyaging from the port is matched by inward-looking streets, hidden gardens, stairways that do not seem to lead anywhere. Lisbon is a city of steep inclines and complicated, unsymmetrical streets that criss-cross the hills: only in the Baixa area near the river and in the more modern northern part of the city does any form of a grid system appear.

Foreigners, including the English, added to the vast flow of literature about the city, in the nineteenth century. Julio de Castilho and other writers put 'olisipography', as the study of Lisbon became known, on a scholarly footing. Poets, writers and musicians have enthused over the ages on particular parts of the city – whether it was the *fadistas* singing of the Alfama, the Romantics languishing at the sight of the moon on the Tagus or Fernando Pessoa stalking the streets of the Chiado. All these perceptions of the city are part of its identity, part of its existence in the imagination of those who perceive it. Exploring them will bring us closer to understanding the enduring character of Lisbon.

Lisbon, as Queen of the Seas, claims for herself
dominion over so much of the ocean as extends
from the mouth of the Tagus to Africa and Asia
in an immense maritime circuit.

Damião de Góis

City mournful and gay, once more I dream in you.

Fernando Pessoa

I say 'Lisbon'
When I arrive from the south and cross the river
And the city opens up as if born from its name.

Sophia de Mello Breyner

From Mythical to Medieval City

The evolution of Lisbon from prehistoric times through to the Middle Ages can be seen as a series of phases in the life of the city, each of which has left a significant mark on its character. The first of these stages is the very ancient and indeed elaborately fabled city of pre-classical origins. It is a period shrouded in myth as well as the time when primitive settlements first grew up around the Tagus estuary. The next was the Roman *imperium* during which Lisbon not only became part of a world empire but also became a Latinized city, pre-eminently through its adoption of a vernacular version of Latin. When the Roman Empire collapsed into barbarism, Lisbon joined the league of Christian kingdoms of Iberia, which were to be overrun by the Moorish invasion of the eighth century. Although few physical relics of this period survive, it was important as the time when the Church became established as a leading institution in the city before the Muslim invasion of the eighth century. The establishment of the Moorish caliphate had a profound effect on the city, not only in introducing sophisticated science and technology into its crafts and administration but adding something languid and Eastern that has remained in its character and can still be savoured in the very air of the Alfama district. Four centuries later, in the twelfth century, Lisbon was captured by Portugal's first king, Afonso Henriques, and Christianity was restored. The city expanded considerably into a cosmopolitan, commercial port from which the exploration of entirely new worlds overseas in America, Africa and Asia began. That exploration, in turn, enabled the even more spectacular growth of the city as the leading trading centre of Europe in the early sixteenth century.

The earliest accounts of Lisbon, as of other ancient European cities, are to be found in Greek legend, often vague and obscure.[1] The abiding story, recounted over the ages, is that the city was founded by Ulysses when he travelled westward to the extreme ends of the known world where the fabled gardens of Hesperides were thought to be located. Ulysses must have made his discovery on one of his many voyages after the Trojan War, a period conveniently shrouded in myth and make-belief.

Equally convenient for those wanting to believe in legend, the hinterland of Lisbon, particularly the fertile valley of Colares and the mysterious Mons Lunae or Sacred Mountain at Sintra, was just the right setting for the enactment of heroic deeds. Here were all the physical ingredients of myth: a fertile valley where fruit abounded, a river winding its way to the sea, in the background wooded, green slopes, the perfect repose for nymphs. In this same, Poussin-like landscape, Heracles is said to have battled with a monster that rampaged on the coast. When the god had done his work, the grateful inhabitants dragged the body of the monster away in hefty chains.[2] Nearby, the lofty Cabo da Roca, at the rocky land's end and often swirling in mists, provided the ideal setting for worshipping the gods who were said to pass by the Cape during the night.[3]

The Renaissance Portuguese writers of the sixteenth century, who sealed the story of Ulysses' foundation of the city, did not worry unduly about the exact moment when he arrived on the shores of the Tagus. Camões, the epic poet of the nation whose *Lusiads* (1572) tells the story of the Portuguese exploration of the sea routes to India, says, almost in passing, that Lisbon was

> Named for her founder, that coiner of words
> Through whose cunning Troy was burned
> And the city was founded by Ulysses on the exact spot
> Where the Tagus mingles its fresh water
> And white sands with the salt sea.[4]

Camões' passing reference to the myth was taken up some 50 years later in the monumental work of Gabriel Pereira de Castro, *Ulisseia* (1636).[5] Pereira de Castro was an eminent lawyer who had been a professor at Coimbra. He had written weighty tomes on law and the constitution but clearly yearned to achieve literary, rather than academic, fame. His work, another epic, was intended to adapt Homer's *Iliad* to the Portuguese experience, balancing Camões' evocation of Virgil's *Aeneid* in the *Lusiads*. Like Camões, Pereira de Castro celebrates the feat of overseas discovery by the Portuguese explorers, choosing the lofty heroic mould to set the seal on Portuguese nationhood once and for all. Pereira de Castro's Ulysses arrives at a place where ships may put in safely at harbour[6] and, once ashore, finds its favourable hinterland, fertile in fruit and capable of supporting good agriculture. This is the same Arcadian land that Ulysses was said to have found at nearby Sintra and Colares.

The area in which these myths have been set coincides with the area where the oldest evidence of human habitation has actually been found.[7] A plan reconstructing the Paleolithic and Neolithic dwellings in the City Museum (Museu da Cidade) shows a concentration of population to the north and west of the existing city, slightly away from the estuary of the Tagus itself. The Museum's plan traces sites that may go back 150,000 years. That dating suggests that the area was inhabited by Neanderthal man prior to the arrival from Africa of *Homo sapiens*, now dated about 35,000 years ago.[8]

Definitive evidence of human habitation in Portugal goes back to a much more recent period. At the Coa Valley, in north-central Portugal, occupation has been dated to about 25,000 years ago. The remains there cover an area of about 17 kilometres of valley; the evidence points to the existence of Stone Age cave-dwellers who survived by hunting wild animals such as bison, bull and stag. Images of these animals, and others, are engraved on the walls of caves. Engravings of this kind have been found closer to the Lisbon area in Upper Alentejo. At Escoural near Evora, engravings of bison, horse and curious hybrid creatures, partly human, have been dated to about 20,000 years ago.[9] They show that these cave-dwellers were concerned with representing their environment and trying to interpret the forces that appeared to govern it. The whole area is also rich in Megalithic remains of a more recent period when agriculture and stock raising were well established.

Prehistoric stone structures (dolmens and cromlechs) may be seen at Guadaloupe which date from about 4000 BC. The cromlech at Almendres, standing in a clearing of cork oaks, consists of up to 95 granite monoliths arranged in an oval pattern; at Valverde the anta of Zambujeiro is part of a funerary monument consisting of a gallery and dolmen full of relics, now transferred to the nearby museum. Monuments and relics of the Alentejan type are found in the immediate area of Lisbon. Tombs were typically covered with a removable stone slab so that further bodies could be interred in them.

Just as the benefits of the hinterland were important in the mythical foundation story so in real life they were important to the survival of Stone Age man. First and foremost in importance was the plentiful supply of water – streams and founts are found all over the hills and dales of the city area. The hills themselves provided good defensive sites; there was an abundant supply of fuel in the form of wood. The forests were also the home of wild animals – stags and bison – which became an important source of food for early man.

Nearby the river provided another kind of food, fish, which entered and remained in the national diet.[10] Taking to the water also proved to be a convenient method of transport between communities dispersed along the shores of the estuary and the coast.

There is a substantial collection of remains at the City Museum dating from this early period. Seashell waste, found in the Tagus Valley, suggest that there was already a settlement in the area from the period between 7000 BC and 5000 BC.[11] There are examples of storage jars, vessels of every shape and size, statuary objects, kitchen utensils and, from a later period, ceramic works of various types. By this time the kiln had been invented; flint sickles and hoes were in use; a form of loom has also been found. Funerary remains of various types, indicating a mix of cultures of the indigenous inhabitants, continue to be found.[12]

Gradually the objects show greater decorative sophistication, such as a small dagger-like plate cut in the shape of a fish and marked with rings and circles, or large plates with various ridges and circular decorations. Considerable evidence of similar human settlement has been found in the Sintra area, particularly in the valley of São Martinho to the north of the town and in Estefania. Metal objects suggest occupation during the Bronze Age, when axes and primitive chisels were made. This was the period when a plethora of tribes occupied central Portugal, later known as the Roman province of Lusitania.

A.H. de Oliveira Marques suggests that this was a period of violent conflict when invaders – Lusitanian, Carthaginian and Greek – added to the turmoil of the fighting that was already taking place among the local Iberian tribes.[13] Knowledge of this time is still sketchy but it can be dated from about 1000 BC. Celtic influence was strongest in the north but would have permeated the south as well, a fact already noted by Pliny, who had served in Iberia as Proconsul in the first century AD. The Celts were skilled in iron, bronze and gold work; they brought considerable sophistication to the ancient indigenous worship of the solar and lunar deities said to have been practised at the Cabo da Roca. Their *castros* or hilltop settlements were scattered throughout the territory. In many areas they were built on the sites of already existing prehistoric structures. In turn the Romans and then the Moors built upon the same fortress locations.

Greek and Phoenician communities were already clustered around the coastal areas, with considerable agriculture carried out in the hinterland. Phoenician Olisipo dates from 1000 BC or even earlier, as remains found in the area of Sé Cathedral show. The Phoenician traders, who dealt in gold, silver and tin, brought with them a culture of the sea and a new cosmopolitanism, based on extensive trading links which covered the entire Mediterranean area. They were succeeded by the Carthaginians, another maritime people who controlled most of the North African coast and the strategic Straits of Gibraltar.

Strabo, in his *Geography*, written in the last years of the first century BC, alludes to the fierceness of the Lusitanians and to the considerable prosperity of Tartesso or Megalithic Lusitanian society, which was politically, as well as economically, sophisticated. He contrasts the prosperity of the central southern region with other parts of Iberia, where mountainous terrain or more extreme climate makes for more difficult cultivation and, with it, less economic development and contact with the outside world.

This first 'golden', quasi-mythical age of Lisbon ended quite abruptly when, in 218 BC, the Roman legions marched into Iberia, beginning a colonization that was to have a profound cultural impact, which has endured to modern times. The Roman invasion was part of the global struggle between Rome and Carthage; Rome was determined to dislodge the Carthaginians from the entire area of the Western Mediterranean. Ironically, in areas where the cosmopolitan influence of Carthage was strongest, such as in the central province of Lusitania (in which the district of Scallabitanus covered the Tagus estuary and the Sintra area) assimilation of Roman culture was least difficult. Here the local Lusitani tribe was interbred with Celts and the Conii. The Celtiberians, as they are known, had established important trading links with North Africa, enjoying considerable prosperity, which was partly the result of a rich agriculture practised on the plains between the Tagus and the Douro. They were ensconced in impregnable circular fortresses on strategically linked hilltops. Their livelihood came mainly from pastoral agriculture.

Nevertheless the Romans could not properly control Lisbon and the vital Tagus estuary, which linked it to the sea and southward to the Mediterranean without subduing the considerable local resistance of the Lusitanians, a fiercely independent, martial people. Their leader, Viriatus, organized an effective resistance to Roman occupation, preventing a total Roman takeover for nearly a decade. He was only defeated by an act of treachery among his own men, bribed by Roman gold. Viriatus' death in 139 BC was a serious setback for the Lusitani. It heralded the beginning of the second phase of Lisbon's early history as a city, although the struggle to remain independent of Roman rule was by no means over.

Both Strabo and Diodorus Siculus record a fierce resistance that the Lusitanians put up against further Roman encroachment, with renewed campaigns in 80–72 BC. This time the leader came from a very different social background, being none other than the 'hero' Sertorius.[14] Sertorius was a Roman general, based in Lisbon, who became a champion of the Lusitanian tribe. On account of his political stance he had been driven into exile but returned from North Africa to lead the campaign against Lucius Cornelius Sulla. Sertorius was assassinated in 73 AD but his action held up Roman occupation. Nor did the Roman *imperium* ever properly extend to Trás-os-Montes, which, as always, remained cut off from mainstream developments. Lusitania did not formally become a Roman province until 25 AD, although long before that the southern areas of modern Portugal had become Latinized.

The Romans had invaded Iberia for commercial reasons and to challenge the Carthaginian base in the south of Spain. They had not been concerned, at least initially, with conquering territory, and whilst introducing a centralized administration they were tolerant of local customs and even of local religion. J. Cardim Ribeiro suggests that in Lusitania the worship of the Emperor coexisted and was mingled with the traditional worship of lunar and aquatic deities.[15] Pagan cults of the serpent and the lizard continued covertly for some generations. To these indigenous practices were added Roman cults of Jupiter, Diana and Saturn. *Ex votos*, dedicated to these gods, have been found in various sites in the city. Such mixtures of culture were typical of cosmopolitan, far-flung empires, something which Portugal as a nation would itself experience in later times.

As Roman occupation continued, particularly during the *Pax Romana*, the period which began with the reign of Augustus Caesar in the last part of the first century BC, Lusitania, like other parts of the Empire, flourished. This was a period of administrative con-solidation, during which Roman law was increasingly applied and coinage, standards of weights and measures and the Julian calendar became widely used. The introduction of Latin as the *lingua franca* meant easier conditions for trade and business; at the same time, the infrastructure was improved by the building of roads between vital points in the country. Olisipo, facing the sea and the southern trade routes to North Africa, was at the centre of the Roman network as it had been of the Phoenician trading routes. By the time the Roman grip on Iberia was consolidated, Rome had become mistress of the Mediterranean, having finally destroyed Carthage in 146 BC. Trade routes from the western part of the Empire could now be securely guaranteed. In 138 BC Decimus Junius Brutus undertook reinforcement of the walls of Olisipo, suggesting that the area to the north, inhabited by Celtiberians and Lusitanians, remained hostile to Roman occupation. Meanwhile, the city itself and the entire region continued to prosper, its links being directly to the emperor rather than through the Senate as was usually the case in the administration of Roman provinces outside Italy.

This economic expansion had a considerable effect on the immediate hinterland, based on the export of agricultural products such as olive oil, wine, salt and fish products, particularly the fish condiment of garum, produced in Setúbal, which was exported directly to Rome by sea. Another, more modest source of wealth came from mining for silver and lead. Although the Romans kept the greatest wealth for themselves, there was also opportunity for indigenous inhabitants to prosper. The Romanized Lusitanians, now speaking the local version of Latin which eventually became Galaico-Portuguese, tended to come from the *decuriones*, or middle-class property owners distinguishable from the *senatores* or Roman aristocratic administrators but considerably above the *plebs* or ordinary citizens. Service in the Roman army could lead to membership of the *equites*, a class just below the senatorial class from which advancement to the very highest social rank was a possibility. In Olisipo citizens had the same rights as their Roman counterparts.[16] Gradually local people, including Greeks who were long settled in the city, would also be admitted to the public service, eventually taking up even the important magisterial positions. As in other parts of the Roman Empire, the entire economic system depended on the institution of slavery. The slaves, drawn from the indigenous population, had no rights of citizenship, yet they were the source of cheap labour on which the prosperity of all well-established citizens, Roman or Luso-Roman, depended.

Evidence of the local prosperity in Roman times is spread across the Lisbon region, particularly in the form of funerary monuments. Several of these can be seen in the City Museum's collection, including lapidary remains found in the grounds of the castle of São Jorge. One such records that Voluscia Tusca, daughter of Gaius, lies buried beneath. Another sarcophagus, decorated with an elaborate frieze, is inscribed with the name of a member of the Galeria tribe, one of the most populous in Roman times. Another is inscribed with the gloomy words 'Everything earthly is destined to go.' Inscriptions to the emperor are found on numerous lapidary remains. Other remains also show the extent of sophistication of Olisipo as a city – fountains, temples, theatres, public baths, houses with efficient drainage systems – were features of this well-to-do Roman town. To the east were cemeteries; one necropolis was in the area of São Domingues monastery.

Temples built in the centre of the city were dedicated to the gods Jupiter, Diana and Cybele (around whom grew the cult of the eternal mother – of earth itself). In some cases Christian churches were later built upon these ancient sites – under the floors of Sé Cathedral, layers of the remains of ages have been uncovered.[17] The Christian church was built on what was the patio of the Moorish mosque, which, in turn, straddled a Roman street, with walls and drains on its sides. All these places of worship had been located in highly urbanized settings, close to densely populated areas. Diana's temple was in the forum, somewhere in between the estuary and the ridge on which São Jorge's castle still dominates the skyline. A Roman theatre was located in the Rua da Saudade, running up to the castle walls. A lintel marked 'Main Entrance' was excavated recently. A mixture of local marble (from the Sintra area) and Italian marble from Carrara has been identified in the remains. A stone's throw away is the present-day Taborda Theatre, established in the nineteenth century. The continuous production of theatrical events in such a confined geographical area over the millennia provides a striking example of the continuity of certain features of civic life. Below the ramparts of the citadel, the centre of the present city remained semi-rural with gardens and orchards still reflected in its modern street names.

The Roman city was also well supplied with water, an essential resource for Roman urban life. Drinking water and water for thermal baths were brought to every part of the city by a subterranean system. Given Lisbon's hilly terrain, that was no mean engineering feat. Evidence of the system has come to light over the centuries – after the earthquake of 1755 and much more recently following excavations for the building of the metro in the Praça de Figueira in 2000. A vast cemetery was uncovered underneath the square, with numerous epigraphic inscriptions on the stonework. During excavations pieces of Roman ceramic plate were dug up with other more ancient fossils, indicating continuous inhabitance of the Baixa area since earliest times. In the castle walls and at the Casa dos Bicos, the remains are ornate, displaying all the hallmarks of sophisticated art. A series of streets crossed the city from west to east. At Rossio one of the signal points, which were placed strategically across the urban area, has been uncovered. This was already an area of dense population, as it has remained, with a population of about 30,000.

The Roman *imperium* in Iberia was challenged early in the fifth century at the same time as Alaric the Visigoth sacked Rome (410 AD). The Germanic invasions of the Peninsula began in 407, according to Oliveira Marques, and were made by sea as well as by land.[18] They coincided with considerable local disturbances (*bagaudas*) which had already upset the calm of Roman centres in the north such as Braga. There is evidence that the local insurgents collaborated with the invaders. Nevertheless, although these barbarian incursions compromised Roman control, they did not altogether threaten the Roman way of life, particularly in the towns and cities. The invaders were more interested in the benefits of a rich southern agriculture than in attempting to replace existing political and administrative institutions. Nor had they come in numbers sufficient to displace the indigenous populations. Instead they looked to the fertile soils of the northern parts of Iberia, including areas of what is now northern Portugal and Galicia, as good productive land from which they could make a comfortable living. In due course they moved south, toward the Lisbon area, but tended to avoid direct conflict with the inhabitants of the towns.

Olisipo itself was by now a well-established Roman town with the usual benefits of municipal planning and infrastructure. Its prosperous citizens spread themselves across the whole area, building villas in the *planalto* or flat plain north-westwards toward Mafra. These patterns of civic life firmly identify Lisbon as a Latin city – the cultural heritage of the Roman period (which was largely assimilated by barbarian invaders) sprung roots which endured for much longer than the mere physical buildings of the city, though the evidence suggests these were impressive. Something profound and lasting had been superimposed on the complex, cosmopolitan Phoenician and Greek city by the long period of Roman occupation.

During the fifth century the Suevi occupied Portugal whilst the Vandals and Visigoths invaded Spain. The Suevi, who had come from the Rhineland, were a warrior people who had been constantly on the move and were now tempted to settle in the gentle Luso-Galician lands they had reached. This area of the north-western Peninsula had already formed something of a distinct cultural region toward the end of the Roman period. The capital of the Suevic kingdom was established at the regional centre of Braga (Dume) with occupation of Oporto, further south as well. Much of the information about the Suevic kingdom comes from Hydatius, Bishop of Chaves, who acted as a negotiator between the Suevi and the Romans. He also had dealings with the Visigothic Kingdom of Spain. There was also much turbulence during this period; Roman Conimbriga, for example, was destroyed.

The Suevi did not attempt to obliterate Roman custom where they existed, nor did they change the *lingua franca* of this part of Iberia. Their own language had, in any case, never been written down. The consolidation of their base in the north contributed to the growing identity of that area, which eventually became the foundation of the nation of Portugal itself. When they moved further south, they practised the same policy of tolerance and alliance with the localized Roman communities. The Roman governor of Olisipo, one Lusidius, welcomed Suevic leaders to the city and formed an alliance with them. Nevertheless his efforts did not prevent a sacking of the city in 469.

These political developments encouraged the assimilation of Suevic and Roman culture at a time when Roman rule itself was collapsing. By 476 the Western Roman Empire went into extinction. The pattern of cultural integration which marked its passing was an early example of a toleration of foreigners that has been the common experience of the inhabitants of the Portuguese territory. That toleration continued under Moorish rule, where, in accordance with Koranic imperative, considerable tolerance was shown to believers of other religions, including Christianity and Judaism.

As the relics of Roman administration disappeared, the Catholic Church emerged as the leading political institution; the Suevic Kingdom in Portugal was becoming Christianized, after more than a century of contact with Christian subjects within its jurisdiction. But it was with the arrival of St Martin at Dume, before 550, that the official conversion took place. St Martin is said to have saved the life of the son of the Suevic king, Theodemir, and, perhaps as a reward, was duly installed at Braga as archbishop. At Dume he rebuilt the church dedicated to his namesake, St Martin of Tours, who in the Middle Ages was to become a great cult figure after whom many churches were named. St Martin had the vision of a secular kingdom but one that was Roman in its religion and culture. It would also have the capacity to absorb pagan features in its ritual. The authority of the Church was confirmed by the holding of religious councils at Braga in 563 and again in 572. The result of these councils was a reorganization and strengthening of the Church by the rearrangement of sees and synods, both within the Suevic kingdom and in neighbouring Galicia. These developments confirmed a cultural identity for the northern region which was later to prove decisive in the formation of the kingdom of Portugal.

St Martin's political views were later reflected in the code of St Isidore of Seville, which similarly aimed to apply a system of law to Romans, Suevi and Goths alike. Within these basically theocratic states, commerce was considered to be a morally dubious activity. Its practice was left to the Jewish minority. As in other parts of Europe, the exclusion of Jews from the professions meant that they became dangerously marginalized from mainstream society. Nevertheless, they were left to practise their own religion until the Inquisition was set up in the sixteenth century. Occasionally things were less welcome to the citizens of Ulixbuna (as Lisbon had become known), such as the tribute demanded after a Visigothic invasion. The Visigothic kingdom in Spain and the Suevic kingdom in Portugal survived as theocracies until the invasion of the Moors at the beginning of the eighth century. While the physical relics from this period in Portugal are few, the establishment of the Church as a political institution of significance in the affairs of the city was something that would prove enduring and would be restored after the next phase of Muslim occupation, which was to last for four centuries.

The Moorish period began with the tentative crossing of Moorish troops from North Africa in 710 under the command of Tarif Ibn Malik. The purpose of his mission was to test what resistance there might be to Muslim annexation of lands reputed to be rich in human and natural resources. The Moorish invaders were surprised not to meet any local opposition; Tarif Ibn Malik reported back to the governor of Tangier, Tarif Ibn Ziyad, that a full-scale invasion was feasible. This took place the following summer in 711 under the governor's own command. Late in the day, the Visigothic king, Roderick, who had been campaigning against the Basques in the north, realized the danger. He returned to Córdoba and rallied what he could of a mixed band of Iberian troops. By this time, the Moorish army had had time to ensconce itself at Algeciras where it waited. When Roderick was at last ready to attack, which he did, his divided forces could not match the discipline of the invading army. The Christian coalition was roundly defeated; within a matter of months, the Moorish generals swept northwards, taking Seville, Mérida and Toledo on the way. The territory of Portugal was in Muslim hands by 713; the Moors were led by Abelaziz Ibn Musa, the son of Tariq Ibn Malik.

These Moorish incursions began a chapter of immense significance in the history of Iberia. Although the territory of Portugal began to be 'liberated' in the twelfth century, Moorish rule on the Peninsula as a whole lasted until the end of the caliphate in Granada in 1492. It was not, of course, a period of continuous calm. Local resistance to Moorish rule began within a decade of the foreign arrival and in the far north of Spain and in difficult, mountainous territory in the north of Portugal, the rule of the Moorish rulers was shaky, and in part non-existent. Christian states like Asturias were established in the north and the caliphs of the south had to mount an annual summer campaign against the Christians to protect their precious Iberian territories. Sometimes alliances formed across the religious divide in recognition of the fact that the Moorish presence in Al Andalus was the most politically significant in the Peninsula.

Moorish rule affected Iberia in many different ways: Lisbon, at the western point of the Peninsula, shared that experience as much as other Iberian cities. One of the abiding cultural legacies of the occupation, particularly in the earlier centuries, was that of cultural and indeed ethnic mixing. The attitude of the Muslim rulers was based on a religious precept but undoubtedly was shaped by pragmatic considerations as well. The Koran teaches a respect for all religions (including Christianity and Judaism) whilst the small number of the Moors in proportion to the indigenous population (estimated at between 40,000 and 300,000) suggested the wisdom of a liberal system of governance.

Nevertheless peaceful integration was not always possible. The threat from the Christian kingdoms of the northern part of Iberia was matched by internal insurrection. From time to time dangerous, radical sects appeared, as in 944, leading to their suppression and an anti-Christian mood. The arrival of the puritanical Almovarids, toward the close of the eleventh century,

ended the policy of tolerance altogether. The fusion of culture and
religion so characteristic of Mozarab Balata, in which Lisbon was
situated, was to be severely tested. By the time of the so-called
Reconquest,[19] the tradition of tolerance between religions had
entirely died.

Moorish rule in the Garbe (as the Portuguese caliphate was
known) was concentrated on the south (the area of modern Algarve) with the city of Silves as its capital. The southern part of
the country had become very populous, rivalling centres in the
north. But like their predecessors, the Suevi and the Romans, the
Moors were content to build upon local structures and, where it
made sense, to amalgamate customs and practices with their own.
The Roman *territorium* or province was replaced by the Moorish
kura; the *conventus* or constituency by the *qarya*. The feeling
of administrative continuity added to a gradual assimilation of
Christians to Moorish rule and the development of a distinctive,
mixed Mozarab culture.

The cultural and economic significance of the Moorish occupation of Balata, the province that stretched from Lisbon to
Santarém, was considerable. Not only were practical sciences like
irrigation effective in raising agricultural production but Portuguese culture was influenced by the language, law and customs
of Islam in many different ways. The most graphic examples of
this influence was in architecture, as was the case across Iberia
and in the art of ceramics which remained a main form of artistic
expression when Portugal eventually emerged as a Christian nation
in the twelfth century.

Lisbon was always the jewel in the crown of Moorish Balata – a
series of fortresses at Santarém and at Sintra formed a protective
ring around the capital. This protection was much needed since
there were a number of Christian attempts to take the city. It was
attacked in 796 by the King of Asturias and in 844 by the Normans
from the sea but a stout resistance saw off the enemy. It was sacked
again by Spanish forces in 851. Another Norman invasion, centred

on Alcácer do Sal, was defeated in 966. In the eleventh century the city was taken by the Christians, but was recaptured by Sid Ibn Abu Bakr in 1094 when Count Raymond of Burgundy was defeated outside the city's smoking walls. In addition there were various internal Arab uprisings, sometimes led by disaffected Berbers, from the earliest times.

The hinterland of Lisbon, particularly in the fertile area of Colares and around the estuary of the Tagus, benefited from the sophistication of Moorish irrigation systems and methods of water storage. Wheat and barley, vegetables and fruit (including the grape) were grown in these areas adjacent to the city. Despite the Koranic injunction against drinking alcohol, the vine continued to be cultivated as it had been in Roman times. Ibn Muçana, mayor of Lisbon in the eleventh century, penned his ode to Alcabideche, then a small village in the footholds of the Sintra hills, praising among its products grain, onions and pumpkins.[20] He and other Moorish poets enthused on the luxuriant vegetation which a plentiful supply of water allowed, as well as a rich wildlife which included much prized falcons.

The Moors were also responsible for rebuilding much of the city, which had fallen into ruins in Germanic times. The citadel of São Jorge, its rampant walls and all the main defensive structures of the modern city were put in place; a medina, mosques, fountains and governor's residence were all constructed to embellish the city; ceramic arts of tiling and roofing were introduced. The area of Alfama just below the walls of São Jorge's Castle, with its maze of winding streets, white houses and small hidden gardens or interior courtyards, is the most notably Moorish area. The castle was itself the seat of Moorish rule – the Alcáçova, as it was known, continued to be the principal residence of the early Portuguese kings. The Alfama itself is an inward-looking quarter: blank walls face streets which twist in complicated patterns; cobbled staircases descend steeply into obscure alleyways. There is always a surprise awaiting – either a sweeping vista or a dead end can greet the walker when turning a corner. The quarter lies protected by the shadow of the castle walls above it.[21]

The mood of Moorish Lisbon is well caught in José Saramago's novel *The History of the Siege of Lisbon*, which tells the story of the city's capture from the Moors in 1147 by Afonso Henriques, the first king of Portugal and known as the Conqueror. Here is an early morning scene of what could be an Islamic city anywhere across the Muslim world:

> Much, much later, the first light of morning broke through behind the city, black against the light, little by little the minarets faded, and when the sun appeared, still invisible from this spot where we are standing, familiar voices could be heard echoing amongst the hills, those of the muezzins summoning the followers of Allah to prayer.[22]

One of Saramago's turbanned muezzins is blind. Hearing the sound of rejoicing, he wonders if the infidels have been defeated by a response from Allah, who has heard the fervent prayers of the devout citizens and sent the angels Munkar and Nakir, guardians of his tomb, to exterminate the Christians.[23] As Saramago shows, the defence of Lisbon rested upon the rampart fortifications, with São Jorge's Castle at the high point on the ridges, the only access to the city from the north and east being through three gates of Martim Moniz, of Sol and of the Alfama itself. On the southern side was the gate of Alfofa, access to which was well-nigh impossible due to the precipitous rock faces rising from the estuary in front of it. Moreover from any point along the river, the invaders would have to cross difficult terrain to actually get to the bottom of these natural ramparts in the first place. Seen from their perspective, the city appeared as one vast impenetrable dome.

The exotic strain of Saramago's account of the end of the Caliphate in Lisbon reflects a profound influence that the period has had in the imagination of the nation. Although the Christian reconquest has been traditionally seen as the resurgence of the Christian nation, the events that took place need to be set in the context of a rich, cross-cultural society which, in its cosmopolitan adoption of more than one set of norms and customs, set the scene for a country which was to become comfortable in overseas and far-flung lands. Centuries of Mozarabic life were not flung aside but synthesized into the fabric of the new nation.

At the head of this new revolution was the dashing figure of Afonso Henriques, a Burgundian prince who failed several times to take Lisbon either in 1137 or in 1140 on his second attempt. His campaigns, extending over several decades, were aimed at securing the northern territory of Portucale, the embryo of the Portuguese kingdom, soon to be recognized by Rome. When he did succeed in capturing Lisbon in 1147, seven years later, he had to rely on the support of a motley collection of English, German and Flemish mercenaries. The foreigners did not support him for nothing; their eyes were on the considerable spoils that Lisbon would have to offer. Rumour had it that great wealth had been amassed in the city by its Moorish rulers. This was the glittering prize the crusaders fought for.

A propaganda war was also fought on both sides. The Archbishop of Braga rallied the Christian side. He railed against the Moorish inhabitants of the city.

> Go back unbidden to the land of the Moors where you came, with your luggage, money and goods and your women and children, leaving to us our own... You Moors and Moabites fraudulently seized the realm of Lusitania from your King and ours.[24]

The Moors were not impressed. They had occupied the city for centuries; it was clearly God's wish that it should be Muslim. They had no intention of handing it over to infidels. After persistent attempts, English and Flemish troops eventually managed to drive the Moors back from western and eastern suburbs but the defenders, having nothing to lose, ensconced themselves in the citadel, where they fought off further attacks.

The siege lasted over four months; the Moorish garrison was reduced almost to starvation despite beginning with a large underground store of wheat and barley, dried figs and oil.[25] The summer heat made conditions particularly unpleasant. There were rumours of cannibalism having broken out among a population that may have numbered 40,000. The propaganda war was also continued on both sides – the Christians trying to put the fear of God into the defenders, the defenders relying on the will of Allah to protect them. Miraculous events were reported in both camps; heroes such as Martim Moniz were later honoured by having parts of the city named after them. In the end it was the building of attacking towers by the English that enabled troops to storm the citadel. Once the crusading mercenaries breached the defences and entered the city, they indulged in uncontrolled pillage and debauchery – those inhabitants who could fled from the city in fear of their lives; others were massacred.

After the capture of Lisbon by Afonso Henriques, the Muwalladi population (Christians who had converted to Moorish rule) and remaining Moors tended to reside in certain designated areas or *mourarias*. Like the Jews, they were allowed to continue practising their faith without hindrance, although they were stigmatized as second-class citizens debarred from holding civil or military posts. An Englishman, Gilbert of Hastings, gained his reward for serving Afonso Henriques by being installed as the Bishop of Lisbon. A new cathedral, Sé, was built in the grounds of the principal mosque, as we have seen. The rest of the city was divided into nine parishes, each with its own church, of which three – São Vicente, Santa Justa and Nossa Senhora dos Mártires – survive.[26]

The cosmopolitan mix that all this entailed and the city's web of foreign connections meant that the growth of medieval Lisbon as a seaport came as a natural cultural development. From earliest times Lisbon had had a maritime flavour; its experience of many seafaring nations – whether they were Phoenician, Greek or Roman – brought a wealth of knowledge and expertise in the various arts of navigation and commerce. During Moorish times one of the city gates opened directly on to the sea. Legend also played a part in the growing maritime identity of Al-Usbana or Moorish Lisbon.

One story told of the embarkation of eight young voyagers who set sail to find the limits of the world. Whether they returned or not is unknown but the same quest was undertaken hundreds of years later by the Portuguese explorers of the Manueline Age. The notion that Lisbon had connections with the most distant places in the world was already part of its fabric, mythical and real.

The importance of the sea to Lisbon was marked in the growth of naval activities and installations, on the one hand, and the protectionist policies adopted towards fishing, on the other. Small single-mast boats were gradually replaced by more sophisticated, larger vessels of three masts. Eventually the caravel, swift and much admired abroad, enabled exploration of the far-off West African coast. Naval carpenters and shipwrights were awarded special privileges above other trades such as armourers or tailors[27] so that the industry connected to the sea continued to attract recruits. Meanwhile, long-distance fishing and the preservation of fish by salting became part of the city's life. By the fourteenth century Portuguese merchant shipping was established all over Europe. In the Low Countries factories were set up at Bruges and at Antwerp. There was a direct trading link to London. By the end of the century Lisbon had become a bustling seaport with 400 or 500 ships using the facilities of the harbour. The city lay strategically placed between Europe and Africa and, eventually, between Europe and America. Among the cargoes carried out of the port were those of cork, olive oil, wine, hides, wax and honey whilst metals, arms and textiles were imported.[28] The impetus to sail further, particularly in a southerly direction, came in the next century, by which time the lure of gold and slaves from Africa encouraged further expansion of the Portuguese shipping trade. The new coinage, the cruzado, was minted in 1457.

The growth of Lisbon's maritime trade had many effects, from the development of parts of the city to immigration by particular foreign nationals closely connected with the international commerce. While the area around Rossio continued to grow in

importance, eclipsing the eastern ridges of the castle and the
Alfama, the land adjacent to the sea at the front of the modern
Baixa also expanded. Along the river, the shipbuilders set themselves up; warehouses and naval quarters came later on. Occupy-
ing the littoral involved drainage schemes and the creation of
embankments on the levelled-out land: engineering knowledge
of this type increased as demand led to more developments along
the Tagus estuary. The merchant class and the nobility were the
principal beneficiaries.

We have seen that the English were involved in the earliest
days of the city but another nationality well represented were the
Italians including Lombard merchants, Venetian traders, Milanese
financiers and above all the seafaring Genoese. The Genoese had
already become leading traders in the North Sea and the Baltic:
Lisbon was an obvious port of call on the way southward again to
the Mediterranean via Gibraltar and Ceuta where they were well
established. Genoese merchants were already gaining rights in
the city by the second part of the thirteenth century. Among the
Italian community are mentioned certain Vivaldo brothers, who
had influential connections in their home city.

One Genoese, Manuel Pessagno, became the first Portuguese
admiral of the fleet,[29] eventually taking on a Portuguese name,
Pessanha. In the royal letter of appointment of 1317, Pessagno is
given ultimate authority over all Portuguese vessels. He and his
successors are bestowed with the fiefdom in an act of ultimate
feudal authority by Dom Dinis. Naval development was boosted by
the need to fend off pirates, particularly Moorish ones, who raided
the ships which plied their trade in and out of Lisbon. Pessagno
came from one of the cosmopolitan, mercantile families of Genoa
(his brother was based in England) so he understood very well the
value of protecting trade. In due course he set himself up in style
in a palace on one of the city hills which later became known as
Pedreira. No doubt his presence, as well as that of other Genoese,
added to Portuguese knowledge of cartography, a science that later

was to underlie the explorations encouraged by Prince Henry the Navigator. The Italians also introduced the compass and many improvements to shipping construction.

Another foreign community of significance in Lisbon was the Jewish one. Jews who had fled persecution from different European countries found a reasonable degree of religious tolerance in Portugal. Even so, they were confined to certain areas or quarters (*judiarias*), the oldest of which was right in the centre of the city near Baixa, where their synagogue had been built in the Moorish times. Later other ghettoes were designated, although successful individuals would always manage to live outside them. The magnates wore the same clothes as Christians, unlike their less privileged fellow Jews, who were obliged to wear special identifying marks on their garments. Dr Jeronimo Munzer, on tour in 1492, gives a flavour of the opulence of the city's Jews.

> At the foot of the castle there are three Jewish quarters that close down at night. On the Saturday before St. Andrew's feast, I visited the Jewish synagogue and I must say that I have never seen its equal. In this temple, there is a patio covered by an enormous vine; its circumference measures four palms. The place is lovely and there is a cathedra to preach from, like in the mosques! Inside two large candelabra are lit, with 50 or 60 lamps each, among other lights. Women have a separate synagogue, which is also profusely lit. Lisbon Jews are wealthy; charging handsomely for their services. They treat the Christians with insolence.[30]

The proximity of the Jewish quarter to the business and harbour area of the city underlines the importance of the Jewish merchants in the commercial life of the city. Christians could enter the well-placed Jewish areas to conduct business during the daytime. Whenever royal consideration was being given to moving the Jews to other areas (complaints were made from time to time about the advantages of the Jewish sites), the commercial importance of the community was not overlooked.

The Moorish designated area (*mouraria*) remained closer to the castle walls, in the area north of the Alfama, which we have already noted for its Arabic architectural character. One recurring characteristic of the style was in its use of arches and small, almost hidden windows, a feature which adds a particular charm to the streets of the area. The Moors and Mozarabs retained their mosque, and control of that area was regulated from a council meeting in it. The chief officer was the *alcaide* or mayor; the religious life continued to be regulated by the imams and muezzins who called the faithful to prayers. The Moors too were obliged to wear identifying clothing, for example the half-moon emblem on the turban. Unlike the Jews, the Moors were prohibited from many activities, including commerce, so that they were confined to making a living as artisans or craftsmen or agricultural labourers. Even in these lowly occupations, they were subject to taxation from which the crown benefited.

During the Middle Ages, Lisbon, like other European cities, suffered from the twin calamities of famine and plague. It also had another natural disaster to contend with – that of earthquakes, which hit the region from time to time. In a largely agricultural economy, failure in crop production led to immediate disaster. The cause of bad harvest was usually drought, but from time to time inundation from rain ruined a year's crops. The years 1333 and 1334 were particularly bad – wheat production was all but wiped out and with it the staple diet, bread. Starvation threatened the populous city and people were reduced to eating grass. The plague too took its toll in the fourteenth century; the most serious outbreak was in 1348. It affected countryside and city alike but the effects in the city, already the target of migration by the peasants, were worse. It is possible that between a third and a half of the population of the greater Lisbon area perished in that year. The suffering and hardship were immense.

As well as the proximity of volcanic rock in the Sintra area, a series of seismic fault lines run across in a north-easterly direction from the 'Focinho' or 'muzzle' of the Cabo da Roca. Trembles were often recorded but the two worst occurrences were in 1356 and 1531. Damage to buildings, such as churches, is recorded on these occasions sometimes in the plans for repairs to buildings that needed to be undertaken, sometimes in the plans for complete reconstruction when the damage had been severe. Like all natural disasters, the earthquakes also reinvigorated the economy, providing extra employment for those in the building and construction industry in particular.

Natural disaster was matched by the continued threat from Spain, once the Moorish occupation of the Algarve was brought to an end in the mid-thirteenth century. The military orders of Santiago, as well as the Templars and Hospitallers, had played an important part in this success. By 1256 Lisbon had become the capital of the emerging nation, one of the earliest territorial states of modern Europe.[31] The character of the nation was consolidated by the growth of Galaico-Portuguese as a distinct Iberian dialect. Most legal records concerning the ownership of property and royal charters were originally written in Latin. During the twelfth century, the vernacular is mingled with the Latin records. The growth of national identity, closely linked to language, gained a considerable boost during the reign of King Dinis, who, among other cultural gestures of significance, founded the Estudo Geral or first university in Lisbon, which was then located in the Alfama. In the 1290s the university moved to Coimbra but during the next hundred years or so moved to and fro between the two cities. The university depended on the patronage of the Church as much as of the state; many Portuguese continued to study abroad at institutions like Salamanca or further afield in Montpellier and Louvain. King Dinis ordered the translation of official documents into Portuguese; he, like other members of the Burgundian dynasty, was interested in courtly verse, which was now written in Galaico-Portuguese in Spanish, as well as Portuguese, court circles.

More significant in political terms was the growth of the local councils, whose authority has derived from charters (*forais*) granted to various towns by successive monarchs. Whilst the nobility, with its commitment to military service, headed the hierarchical social pyramid of medieval society, below them were the gentlemen knights (*fidalgos*) and the higher clergy, whose political support was useful to the crown.

Considerable benefits were bestowed upon these worthy citizens in the charters of Lisbon and Sintra; that in turn guaranteed the support of the peasants who worked on the lands of the *fidalgos* or in one way or another were connected to serving the crown. The local councils (later seen by the nineteenth-century historian Alexandre Herculano as developments of the Roman *curia plena* and the Germanic *concilia*) formed the basis of the *cortes* or great council which the King regularly consulted on matters of state. Whilst the first *cortes* called at Coimbra in 1211 consisted of noblemen, the 1254 *cortes* of Leiria was made up mainly of burghers. During the same period, Afonso IV reformed the system of justice, trying to inject a greater impartiality into the judicial process by appointing judges to serve outside the districts from which they themselves came. A hierarchy of higher and lower courts was established. Civil law was distinguished from criminal law.

King Dinis had also taken an active interest in economic development. He understood the importance of ownership of land among smaller holders, encouraging disenfranchisement of larger interests, including that of the Church. To boost national prosperity, he undertook public works such as land drainage and supported mining for silver and iron, continuing to extract the traditional royal tax of a fifth of the value of any production. Meanwhile new orders of chivalry (the Order of Christ at Tomar), and benefits bestowed upon the university and those studying sciences, encouraged the consolidation of the national effort to improve standards of living. Despite this redistribution of wealth, the most cultivatable land remained in the hands of the nobility and clergy.

As communications from north to south of the country improved, the wealth of the towns increased with benefits to the crown, which collected taxes in cash and kind. The court tended to move about the country: both Afonso IV (1325–1357) and Pedro I (1357–1367) moved between Lisbon, Santarém and Coimbra, giving out the idea that the king was a man of all his domains. When Fernando succeeded in 1367, the crown was reputed to have hoarded 800,000 pieces of gold and 400,000 silver marks in the castle of Lisbon alone.[32] It was Fernando's marriage to the Spanish princess Leonor Teles which led directly to unrest in the capital. Henry II of Castile had been seen as the major threat to the city, laying siege to it in 1373 and forcing Fernando to abandon his alliance with John of Gaunt. The English alliance was only revived after the death of Henry but Fernando's pursuit of it showed how it remained an option for combating the Castilian menace as it arose from time to time. To counter the immediate threat, Fernando built a new defensive wall around the city, the 'cerca Fernandina', which was completed in 1376.

The history of these years was chronicled much later by Fernão Lopes, who became the custodian of records at the Torre do Tombo, eventually to become the principal national archive. Lopes was commissioned by Dom Duarte to write his chronicle of Portuguese history in 1434. Known as the *Chronicle of 1419 or the Seven First Kings of Portugal*, it is the principal example of contemporary historiography. Robert Southey, a considerable scholar of the lusophone world, greatly admired Lopes, respecting the chronicler's use of documentary evidence, some of which was subsequently lost. That attention to sources adds to the value of Lopes's work, however ideologically slanted its overall perspective.

Civil unrest reached a climax in 1383 when a group of disaffected burghers approached João, Master of the Order of Avis and bastard son of Pedro I, to take the crown. By this move, they wanted to prevent the accession of Juan I of Castile, whose claim to the Portuguese throne was based on his marriage to Beatriz, King Fernando's daughter. Juan I was supported by many of the old nobility whilst João attracted members of the rising families such as Nun'Álvares Pereira,[33] a young soldier who managed to rally the citizens of Lisbon to the Avis banner. Their support was given on the basis of some political representation – a body known as the 'House of Twenty-Four' was created as part of the political settlement. Each of the twelve major city guilds elected two representatives to the House. In turn members of it attended meetings of the city council, through which there was access to the crown. The Avis dynasty, as it became, was therefore founded on a certain populist basis in so far as the burghers and tradesmen of Lisbon played some part in its establishment.

The contest between the two rival claimants reached a peak when the Spanish invaded Portugal. The Spanish claimant was already unwell and decided to avoid the towns of Coimbra and Leiria. The Portuguese were guarding the Tagus, waiting for English reinforcements. At a crucial moment Nun' Álvares decided to attack the invaders and, marching northwards, met and defeated the Castilians at the battle of Aljubarrota on 14 August 1385. The battle was won partly as a result of the technical prowess of English archers, opening a new phase in the relations between the two kingdoms, which gained formal recognition in the following year by the Treaty of Windsor, 1386. The terms of the treaty stated that

> there shall be between the two above-mentioned kings now reigning, their heirs and successors, and between the subjects of both kingdoms an inviolable, eternal, solid, perpetual and true league of friendship, alliance and union.[34]

The treaty bound the two countries to come to one another's aid when attacked by enemies. It became the cornerstone of Portuguese foreign policy for centuries and matured into the oldest alliance between European countries. Meanwhile, in recognition of his victory at Aljubarrota, the king ordered the construction of a church of Santa Maria da Vitória at Batalha, a few miles north of the battleground.

The Iberian connection with England might have been even more direct had John of Gaunt succeeded in his quest for the Castilian crown. As it was, his daughter Philippa came to Portugal as the wife of João I. They set up court at Sintra in the summer months, undertaking considerable work on the old royal palace (Paço Real) in the centre of the medieval village. The king and queen were concerned with establishing a court that sufficiently reflected Portugal's status as a leading player among the nations of Christendom.

Their talented offspring, Duarte (the future king), Pedro and the younger Prince Henry the Navigator, all took the task of modernizing the nation seriously. Pedro toured the countries of Europe in search of scientific knowledge; Prince Henry, by his patronage of navigational science, laid the basis for the exploration of Atlantic islands and the West African coast. Madeira[35] was reached in the 1420s and was put under the personal authority of Prince Henry; the Azores, where Flemish settlers joined the Portuguese, was the next discovery. The Atlantic islands as a whole soon became important suppliers of agricultural products, boosting the commercial development of the port of Lisbon. By 1460, when Prince Henry died, the Cape Verde islands had been captured and the Portuguese caravels had reached the coast of Sierra Leone and were poised to continue southwards to the Cape of Good Hope.[36]

Meanwhile the crown found it necessary to tighten its grip on finances. There had been a long tradition that the king paid noblemen (and sometimes others like the gentlemen knights of Sintra) for their services in defence of the realm. A register was kept at court which showed the rise and demise of families when they changed sides in politics – Nun'Álvares Pereira[37] and the House of Bragança had become an important example of the emergence of the new nobility to whom the Avis kings were indebted. Nevertheless, by the time of King Duarte, it was necessary to revisit the amounts being paid out. A system of reversions to the crown in cases where there was no legitimate claimant to the royal grant was put in place (the so-called *Lei Mental* of 1434). The military orders, such as the Templars and the clergy, were also beneficiaries of royal favours; in the latter case it enabled the king to keep control of appointments which were made on the basis of his recommendations to Rome through the transmission of papal letters. At the same time administrative reforms were introduced; a chancellor was appointed to be in charge of royal finances with undersecretaries regulating different areas of income and expenditure. By these means the economic life of a nation that by now may have numbered a million was gradually being centralized.

During the disturbances of the late fourteenth century, as we have seen, the merchant and artisan classes became more assertive – tailors and coopers were involved in supporting the rise to power of João of Avis. When he held his first *cortes*, there were requests for the preservation of knightly practices in the guild system with its strong hierarchical ordering. The Moors and Jews were excluded from membership, though they had, to a certain extent, a system of their own governance in their allotted ghettoes.

Lisbon itself, with its considerable Moorish and Jewish quarters, continued to flourish. Fernando had built a new wall around the city within which there were still *hortas* or garden areas producing food for consumption, although the main supply came from Sintra and Colares (wheat and fruit are most often cited). The benefits of the city's location were well captured in a late-fifteenth-century visitor's account.

> Half a mile below Lisbon are two hills about a quarter of a mile from each other; through the gorge formed between them, the sea flows in the direction of the mouth of the river up to a distance of fourteen leagues. In some places it is up to three leagues wide, being narrower in others. How fertile and well populated the banks of this stretch of sea are! There is an abundance of olive oil, salt and all the fruits of the earth. Ships are sheltered from even the most violent tempests in Lisbon.[38]

The population of the city may have been upward of 50,000.[39] The Portuguese kings continued to live in the castle – still known by its Moorish name the Alcaçova. The cathedral (Sé) rose on the slopes below and the narrow streets of the Jewish quarter continued along the river's edge in the present commercial Baixa. One of the earliest thoroughfares was the Rua Nova D'El Rey, running parallel to the river, just north of the present Praça do Comércio. Houses were now two- or three-storeyed: shops or artisans' workplaces on the ground level with balconies on the first floors. Although the gardens and even pasturage may have been a relief in the urban setting, lack of proper drainage would have made the city unpleasant, particularly in the summer. Many diarists complained of its filthiness. The local habit of pouring out rubbish into the streets continued to cause annoyance to foreign visitors like William Beckford and Robert Southey in the eighteenth century. Some enduring characteristics of the city's personality cannot be counted among its charms.

The Imperial City

Portuguese overseas expansion reached a zenith during the reign of King Manuel I (1495-1521), whose sobriquet, the Fortunate, celebrates the successes of his era. What had started as a commercially based enterprise turned into an imperial quest. The first trading posts usually straddled coastlines. The settlements had a fort as their nucleus; gradually buildings began to appear around it to support commercial activities. The demand for goods and services that these colonies made from the immediate hinterlands in which they were located grew to such a point that occupation of those areas became essential. Moreover, rivalry from other European powers was keen and meant that the Portuguese enclaves had to be more effectively defended than they could be by the strategic fortresses alone. Dutch and English forces made ever bolder attempts to take over the lucrative trade routes, forcing the Portuguese to build more elaborate defences and take more land around the trading ports.

The flowering of the Manueline empire was based on the steady achievements of the preceding century or more. The first arena of Portuguese overseas operation had been in North Africa at the beginning of the fifteenth century. To capture territory from the erstwhile rulers of Iberia, the Moors, was a mark of singular symbolic significance for the Portuguese crown. Patriotic fervour was at a high pitch, so that young members of the nobility were drawn to support a cause that would, in many cases, cost them their own lives. In 1415 a fleet of 200 ships carrying 20,000 troops set sail from Lisbon to capture Ceuta, strategically placed on the African shore across from Gibraltar. In the face of the invaders' overwhelming military superiority, the Moorish inhabitants of the town gave in without resistance. The town was then fortified into a stronghold guarding the vital Straits of Gibraltar.

After this initial success, Dom Afonso V, known as the African, took his campaign right across Morocco, capturing Alcácer-Ceguer, Arsila and eventually Tangier itself (there had been an earlier attempt to take the town in 1437 which had failed). Portuguese African ambitions ended, some eighty years later, with the capture of Mazagão in 1514; the gradual decline of the North African domains which followed was underlined by the disastrous defeat of Dom Sebastião and the flower of the nobility at Alcácer-Quibir in 1578.

Meanwhile, under the stewardship of Prince Henry the Navigator, maritime expansion into the Atlantic had started another imperial venture, which would prove more lasting than the African conquests. At Sagres, in the Algarve, Prince Henry founded an academy dedicated to navigational science. Myth as much as scientific achievement consolidated the reputation of the school. As one historian has put it,

> it was rumoured that far to the south on a lonely headland in Portugal, something strange was taking place. Ships were being launched into the Atlantic and were coming back with reports of unknown islands, of a huge coastline and of races of men no one had ever seen before.[1]

Prince Henry's programme was ambitious and he managed it with an obsessive attention to detail. The pace he set was relentless;

one achievement spurred him on to the next venture. Nevertheless, the Portuguese did not have it entirely their own way. Traditional enemies were on the trail. The Canary Islands, first declared to be Portuguese, were annexed by the Spanish by 1436. Greater success was achieved elsewhere: Madeira, the Azores and the Cape Verde Islands, as we have seen, were secured by the time of Prince Henry's death in 1460. The first expedition along the West African coast had taken place in 1434, led by Gil Eanes. Each year under the guidance of Henry, the fleet penetrated further and further south, engaging on the way in trade and barter. After Prince Henry's death, some of the exploration was done on a private-enterprise basis, with the state providing naval support, but later, by which time the fleet had reached Senegal and Sierra Leone, the crown once again had taken charge.

Just before the accession of King Manuel, Portuguese merchants had already reached the Niger delta and a flourishing trade in gold, ivory, slaves and spices extended along the length of the Gold Coast. The supply of gold became a major source of wealth for the crown, which imposed a rigid control over the trade. The navy was called upon to fend off raids from the Dutch and the English, who were far from content to leave such a prized trade to the Portuguese alone. An unsuccessful attempt to 'civilize' the Congo by introducing Portuguese customs and culture was one of the more bizarre imperial experiments of the 1490s. The Congolese king converted to Christianity, donned European dress and styled himself as 'Dom João I'.

Meanwhile in the decade before King Manuel's accession, the world's horizons were opened up in both eastward and westward directions. In 1487 Bartolomeu Días rounded the Cape of Good Hope (which he called the 'Cape of Storms'), raising the prospect of a direct sea route to India and the East Indies. Dom Manuel's predecessor, King João II, had been prevented from launching an official expedition to India by the scepticism of his advisers in Lisbon; the *cortes* voted against the proposal. However, King João was not going to be stopped. In 1487, he secretly commissioned Pero da Covilhã and Afonso de Paiva to sail eastwards in search of the fabled kingdom of Prester John. Prester John was believed to be a Christian monarch who ruled in Ethiopia and would be an ally in the struggle against Islam. The alliance was considered crucial to opening up the trade route to India. Covilhã himself made straight for India, arriving a year later, in 1488. He went to Calicut, the centre of the spice trade, and also visited Goa. It was only five years later, in 1493, that he actually reached Abyssinia.[2]

Dom Manuel was even more determined than his predecessor to prove the sceptics wrong. He commissioned an expedition of three ships to set sail under the command of Vasco da Gama in 1497. Da Gama followed a westerly course from the Cape Verde Islands, making towards Brazil before he finally sailed south, around the Cape of Good Hope. In Mozambique, as Camões was famously to celebrate in his *Lusiads*, Da Gama was well received by the Sultan of Malindi, who provided him with a pilot to cross the Indian Ocean to Calicut. His mission, to secure the valuable spice trade for the Portuguese crown, was stoutly resisted by the Arab traders who had been in control of it over the ages. Da Gama persisted, trying to convince native rulers of the benefits of dealing with the foremost European nation.

He returned two years later with half the crew he set sail with and one less vessel. It was said that the masts of the returning ships were sighted from the heights of Sintra entering the Tagus estuary. Da Gama was given a hero's welcome. King Manuel sent word of his achievement around the courts of Christendom, boasting, in a letter of 12 July 1499, of the acquisitions of trading posts and rare cargoes of spices.[3]

Such was Dom Manuel's enthusiasm for further exploration that within a short period he commissioned yet another fleet, this time of 13 ships, to secure the valuable Indian trade. The commander of this considerable flotilla was Pedro Alvares Cabral, a young nobleman. Cabral sailed westwards in early 1500 and reached the shores of Brazil, considered to be part of a larger island rather than part of a new continent. In commissioning Cabral's venture, Dom Manuel was making up for lost ground when Portugal had failed to back the Genoese navigator Christopher Columbus in 1492, giving the Spanish a lead in westward exploration.

One of Cabral's ships was sent back to Lisbon to announce the news of the discovery of this new land, already protected as Portuguese territory under the terms of the Treaty of Tordesillas agreed in 1494 after Columbus's earlier voyage. The Treaty, brokered by the pope, made everything west of longitude 370 degrees west of the Cape Verde Islands Spanish, and east of it Portuguese, although given the vagaries of contemporary cartography that was not an entirely clear demarcation. Although Cabral lost a number of ships on this expedition, he returned to Lisbon with a valuable haul of spices. The imperial trade was beginning to provide substantial returns for the Portuguese crown.

Protection of these overseas interests became the cornerstone of Portuguese foreign policy. The expansion eastwards continued apace – in 1503 the Seychelles were reached; Portuguese ships sailed along the Arabian coast to the Maldive Islands and to the coast of India itself. The Persian Gulf trade was secured by the taking of Ormuz. In 1505 Dom Francisco de Almeida was appointed the first viceroy of India. His principal duty was to secure the spice trade in the interests of the Portuguese crown.[4]

Almeida was succeeded by Afonso de Albuquerque, another one of the great colonial explorers and administrators. There was a certain rivalry between these early captains of India; Albuquerque took the view that the routes eastwards to Malacca needed to be fortified. He made Goa his principal base. He modelled it on Lisbon and it was soon endowed with fine public buildings and grand churches. Goa became the capital of the Eastern Empire. From earliest times, miscegenation (racial intermarriage) was encouraged, so that the metropolis spawned its own Indo-Portuguese population, whose cultural identity has remained distinct until the present. As Albuquerque understood, the security of Goa meant that Portuguese control of the sea routes to the Far East became a viable proposition. Malacca was reached by 1509, the Indonesian island of Sumatra at the same time. Four years later, in 1513, Jorge Alvares was the first Westerner to navigate the Chinese coast. By the middle of the century, Macao off the Pearl Estuary in southern China was leased;[5] by 1571 the Jesuits were established at Nagasaki, and Japan, hitherto closed to foreign commerce, was now opened to Portuguese ships.

Dom Manuel attempted to maintain personal control over these expanding colonial territories. While the cascade of his numerous grand titles – Lord of the Seas, of Arabia, Persia and India – symbolized his imperial role, systematic reform of the administration at home was needed to ensure the proper regulation of trade and the accrual of the taxes and duties due to the crown. Cargoes of precious spices arriving on the waterfront at Lisbon needed to be efficiently transferred for storage in the royal palaces and warehouses. A price-fixing system, ensuring distribution to every part of Europe, was put in place but needed to be efficiently administered. A new class of public officials was drawn from the middle class, which in Lisbon included the Jews of the Baixa. They became pivotal in the business of empire, matching the actual achievements of the explorers, who were mainly drawn from the nobility. Their counterparts were employed in the factories abroad, beginning to create a vast body of colonial servants, some of whom did not return to Portugal at all but stayed overseas to found dynasties there. Top posts, such as governorships, remained royal appointments, ensuring that the king kept a personal grip on colonial policy.

In some cases the king contracted rather than commissioned an individual to advance his interests. From 1512 Jorge Lopes Bixorda was chosen in this way to forward exploration in Brazil. In the first decade of the new century, settlements were made in Pernambuco, Porto Seguro, São Vicente and mostly importantly Bahia (Salvador), which was eventually to become the colonial capital. Colonization of the littoral was helped by the preference of native Indians to live in the interior forests rather than on the coastal plains. Moreover, the land that was occupied by the Portuguese settlers was found to be fertile and the climate less severe than in Africa. Sugar, cereals and exotic fruit and vegetables began to be cultivated in the hinterland around the ports. Wood was a major trading commodity and was exported to Europe. The search for minerals was not, at first, productive. But eventually, when gold was discovered in Minas Gerais, a flourishing culture developed around the old towns with their baroque churches and central squares of stately town houses. In the meantime the slave trade became an important if lamentable source of income, based in the northern city of Bahia, which spawned impressive mercantile mansions.

To ensure the steady supply of wealth to the crown (which continued to collect up to 20 per cent tax on all transactions) Dom Manuel sent an annual flotilla to guard the coastal waters where marauders and armed pirates as well as European rivals waited to intercept Portuguese ships on their way to and fro from Europe. Over the period from 1516 to 1530 this policy kept the shipping routes clear and allowed colonization of the interior to proceed without interference. Occasionally even Dom Manuel made a mistake. His personal dislike of Ferdinand Magellan eventually drove Magellan to the Spanish court in 1517, where he found backing for his famous circumnavigation of the globe.[6]

Dom Manuel took steps to match his status as a leading European monarch by rebuilding his royal residence in Lisbon. He wanted to show, in an ostentatious manner, that Portugal was now the leading nation of Europe, rivalling not only Castile but countries in the north such as Holland and England. It was time to move out of the old palace perched on the Alfama down to the river front, the commercial centre of the thriving port. A considerable space was cleared right on the river's edge in a square known as Terreiro do Paço (the present-day Praça do Comércio).[7] The construction of the new palace – called the Paço da Ribeira – was started in 1500 and completed five years later in 1505. Records of the building project are incomplete; a ground plan has not survived. However, its somewhat austere appearance, remarked upon at the time by the Venetian secret agent Lunardo Masser in 1504, can be seen from contemporary drawings and etchings.[8]

From its inception the palace was understood to be part of a complex of buildings that would symbolize the new, cosmopolitan role that the Portuguese crown played on the world stage. The architect chosen to oversee the building was João de Castilho, who was involved in the building of the Hieronymite monastery at Belém where he had chosen to use the new patriotic, Manueline style. Lack of details in the surviving documents leads us to speculate about the decoration he might have chosen for the palace but it is likely that he would have kept to Renaissance forms and motifs such as the overlay of classical ornament with putti, military trophies and the portrait medallions of Roman emperors. There is a possibility that he may have used the *grotteschi* or classical ornamentation associated with the rediscovered Golden House of Nero or Domus Aurea in Rome, which remained popular in Portugal until the eighteenth century.[9]

Whilst the outside appearance was kept fairly simple and even austere, the inside was filled with luxurious furniture, decorations and paintings in the full cluttered style favoured in courts all over Europe. The scale of the complex was ambitious – with overlapping courtyards, great wings and internal patios forming a dense mass of building. Not only was the palace to serve as the king's residence, but it had to function as an internationally prominent court where foreign diplomats could be received. Of even greater significance was the fact that it had become the administrative centre of the far-flung empire, the focal point for national and commercial interest.

The windows of the palace looked right on to the river; a chapel dedicated to St Thomas was installed within. The northern

courtyard bordered the Casa da India, the centre for the administration and running of the eastern trade. Nearby was the Casa de
Flandres, where the clerks supervised the onward export trade to
the Portuguese factory at Antwerp. In other wings of the complex
were the higher tribunal and the finance department. The money
exchange and the military arsenal abutted the royal buildings.

Within the palace itself, the enormous wealth of the crown was
most evident. According to some authorities, Dom Manuel revived
an old tradition of commissioning portraits of his ancestors to line
the corridors of the antechamber. Chinese ceramics (which the
king much admired) and natural specimens from Africa and Asia
were part of the royal collection. Although the inventory of the
building's contents made in 1522 is incomplete, Flemish paintings
are shown as having been bought, as well as a considerable number
of large tapestries. The tapestries, ordered from Tournai, were
divided into 26 panels celebrating Vasco da Gama's discovery of
the sea route to India. Precise, detailed instructions were given
about the subject matter of each panel. Dom Manuel's commanding position, as king, was underlined by a scene that showed him
giving da Gama his instructions as he set sail from the Tower of
Belém. Although some of the historical detail in the panels was
drawn from the illuminated manuscripts of the *Conquest of India*,
which was in the royal library, the real purpose of the tapestries
was to glorify, in a suitably majestic aesthetic, the achievement of
the crown. They were there to bolster the image of the court as
the leading centre of Europe to all the diplomats and foreigners
who would be in attendance at the Ribeira Palace.[10]

The move of the royal residence to the river's edge had considerable significance for the future development of the city. The
centre of gravity had shifted from the medieval heights to the
Baixa or lower flatland on the seaboard of the Tagus. Building
spread westwards towards Santos where the king built another
palace much admired by Francisco de Holanda.[11] The aristocracy
and merchant class, anxious to maintain a close proximity to the

monarch, began to move into the same area, as did foreigners like Bernard Fechter, an aristocratic Danzig merchant who was in the shipping business. Portuguese *fidalgo* families such as the Teles de Melo, the Tavoras, the Alegretes and Marialvas all built houses along the river; some were placed in the Chiado just up the hill from Cais do Sodré. Whilst these were the residences of the grand old families – such as the Albuquerques – others belonged to merchants (including foreigners) who had grown affluent as the commercial importance of the city increased. While the physical face of the city was being transformed by its commercial activity, Lisbon still relied on agricultural support from its hinterland to remain fed.

Some houses were reputed to be of great luxury, something which could attract royal disapproval if taken beyond the status of the king's palace. One such residence was the Casa dos Bicos (on the site, as we have seen, of ancient Roman remains), where Brás de Albuquerque, the son of the famous viceroy, is said to have lived in a lavish style. Whether the story was exaggerated or not, a rumour had it that an African queen had a hoard of jewellery stored for her in the house. Similar ostentatious, *nouveau riche* features began to appear in decorative effects of other houses in the area.

Meanwhile, Dom Manuel assembled a court, which in scale and glamour matched the imperial status that he coveted for Portugal. The poet Garcia de Resende records in a flowery eulogy that the royal conclave might number as many as five thousand. No other court in Christendom, Resende says, can compare in magnificence and cultivation to the Portuguese. The king showered honours upon the aristocratic *fidalgo* families, whose coats of arms were emblazoned on the ceiling of the Sala dos Brasões, under the royal coat of arms, at Sintra Palace. The nobility and the merchant class of Lisbon, which included foreigners like the Florentine banker Lucas Giraldes, were prospering and began to look for ways of showing off their wealth and status by cultivating a lavish style of living, which included patronizing the arts on a grand scale. Dom Manuel set an example by gathering a glittering array of noblemen, commanders of fleets and merchants and mixing them with artists, musicians and writers at court. If the likes of Da Gama and Albuquerque represented the great men of action, Garcia de Resende, Bernadim Ribeiro, Francisco de Holanda and Gil Vicente represented men of letters and the arts. It was a heady mixture that resembled and was meant to resemble the Renaissance courts of the Italian princes. The imitation of the Italian princely style had been introduced by King João II, Dom Manuel's immediate predecessor. He was a dedicated Italophile and encouraged a more foreign, sophisticated taste to develop among the aristocracy. Andrea Sansovino, the sculptor, was one of the outstanding Italian artists that he lured to Lisbon.

Of the artists and writers, Garcia de Resende was probably the most influential at court.[12] He had been the personal confidant of King João II and became a favourite of Dom Manuel as well. Having the ear of two successive monarchs meant that Resende was in the position to set the tone for cultural life. He chose to do so in a highly cultivated, cosmopolitan manner so that the verse and music of the Portuguese court became accepted in the Spanish courts and further afield in Italy itself. His major literary effort was to gather an anthology of Portuguese verse of the previous hundred years, which, together with Gil Vicente, he produced in the celebrated *Cancioneiro Geral*. He also wrote, in a romantic vein, the famous *trovas* or moving verse on the subject of the death of the Spanish courtier Inês de Castro.[13]

Gil Vicente himself was a less cosmopolitan but no less talented artist than Resende.[14] He hailed from the north of Portugal and the typical sound of the *cantiga*, the popular verse of the villages, was in his ears. If Vicente had had the upper hand in the composition of the *Cancioneiro*, this more populist, indigenous style might have been more pronounced in the collection. In any case Gil Vicente went on to express himself in many genres – from comic farce to serious religious works and allegories in the classical style. His characters too show the sweeping range of his imagination – from recognizably human types to gods and mythological beasts in the classical manner. Sometimes he uses dramatic personification – for example in his *Triunfo do Inverno* (1529) where the *serra* or mountain of Sintra makes an appearance as a character.

Vicente's artistic impulse was to bring vernacular Portuguese into his dramatic and lyrical structures. That concern with the rhythms of early Portuguese has earned him a place in the canon of literary founders of the national culture. The coincidence of his literary intention and a political belief that the drift to Lisbon and the court was depopulating the countryside and undermining its traditional social structure adds a remarkably modern edge to his artistic expression. Nevertheless, Vicente did not fail to pay due respect to the crown – Sintra is described as a terrestrial paradise which was bestowed upon the kings of Portugal by Solomon himself. The House of Avis is thereby given a status usually reserved for the ancient monarchs of Persia and India.

In a court where the pastoral mood was being linked to the philosophical, it is not surprising to find a penchant for the Virgilian eclogue, which could encompass the aesthetic with the social. Francisco de Sá de Miranda was the master of this genre. A native of Coimbra, he had travelled to Spain and Italy, meeting the Neapolitan classicist Sannazaro, whose *Arcadia* (1504) deliberately echoed Virgil, Horace and Ovid.[15] Sannazaro's writing celebrated, in a somewhat idealized way, the pastoral life. His work is replete with shepherds, in idyllic Arcadian settings, accompanied by fauns and nymphs. Sometimes these idealizations were based on marine images, something which reflected the maritime flavour of the incipient Portuguese national mood.

Sá de Miranda, who was courtly as well as cosmopolitan, took his classics seriously. After a bout in Dom Manuel's glittering court, he retired in Horatian manner to his country manor in the Minho where he pursued his classical and literary studies, having a deep empathy with the works of Petrarch and Dante, among others. Like Gil Vicente, Sá de Miranda was also concerned with the independence of Portugal in a court where the Castilian influence threatened dominance. He also shared Vicente's unease about the effect of the pull of Lisbon and the court on the traditional social order. There is a strong suggestion in his work that there is wholesomeness about life on the land which contrasts favourably with the artificial life of the city. Highly stylized and polished, Sá de Miranda also has his place in the development of the national culture.

The last of the prominent Manueline court writers was Bernardim Ribeiro.[16] Sá de Miranda's contemporary and friend, Ribeiro was very much the courtly poet, who lived in a tower of the old Moorish castle at Sintra. His first works appeared in the *Cancioneiro Geral* of Resende, but his most celebrated work, *Menina e Moça*, was only posthumously published in 1554. A contributor to the eclogue form, Ribeiro wrote in Latin, Hebrew and Castilian as well as in Portuguese. His interest in Hebrew and in all aspects of Jewish lore suggests that he may himself have been a new Christian or converted Jew. Adherence to Jewish culture was a dangerous proclivity in an increasingly intolerant religious climate.

Ironically, Ribeiro, like the other court poets, lamented the passing of an idealized, rustic existence. His work is permeated by nostalgia for a lost, Arcadian past; there is a deep melancholy that heralds the Portuguese penchant for regret or *saudades*. But in Ribeiro this lyrical whimsicality is underlined by a philosophical complexity, quite modern in its tone. For Ribeiro is much concerned with questions of identity; as an artist he recognizes a multiplicity of voices within himself and he searches for the 'true' expression of his vision. In this questioning Ribeiro appears very much like a predecessor of the modernists, presaging the mood and tone of twentieth-century writers Mario de Sá Carneiro and Fernando Pessoa. Ribeiro seems to be struggling with the concept of the subconscious centuries before it was defined; his novel is written in the female voice with a distinct psychological undertone. Influenced by the natural setting of the pastoral, the poet is a brooder who tries to make sense of the emotional and philosophical complexities of the human predicament. Dark and mysterious, Ribeiro's mood matches the solitudes of the Sintra mountain where the ancient gods hold sway.

Francisco de Holanda may appear, as the dilettante in this group of heavyweight Manueline courtiers but his influence, as well as learning, always lightly worn, was considerable.[17] Francisco was the son of António de Holanda, a heraldic adviser to the court who had come to Portugal from the Low Countries in the early years of Dom Manuel's reign. Francisco was brought up close to the royal family and in particular was a friend of Prince Luís, with whom he shared a passion for horses. He himself became a favourite of Dom Manuel's successor, King João III, providing miniaturist portraits and specially designed jewellery for the royal family. He was interested in classical art and all things Italian, especially after visiting Rome and catching the eye of the great Michelangelo himself.

Presiding over this rich literary culture, with its artistic interest in classical art and buildings, inclined Dom Manuel to a new sensitivity about buildings, whether they were royal palaces or national monuments. He embarked upon an ambitious programme of building during the course of which a new florid style of Gothic design, much later associated with his name, began to flourish. This so called Manueline style is not easy to define. It is an indigenous mixture of Gothic (which predominated in Portugal well into the period when Renaissance styles had already been established in other parts of Europe) and something more exotic and oriental. The contrast with Greek and Gothic are well caught in Sophia de Mello Breyner's verse.

> The Manueline Style
> Not the Romanesque nave where the rule
> Of seed rises from the earth

> Nor the stalk of wheat
> Of the Greek column
> But the flower of encounters
> That roaming and drift gather[18]

It was a style suited to embellishing and softening the decoration of solid ecclesiastical buildings or castles.

The elaborate sculpturing typical of 'high' Manueline (which evolved during the reign of Dom Manuel and indeed beyond it) typically depicted exotic animals as well as fauna and flora. Columns would be twisted and twined to imitate 'natural' movement; arches would be adorned with mouldings in the form of nautical cables. Ribs of plain pointed arched vaulting are supplemented by heavy liernes in round or square relief; intertwining mariner's knots give bulk to decorative cables. Tritons, sea nymphs and mermaids are used for graphic illustration. Niches and turrets twist and turn in elaborate baroque patterns over doorway lintels. The overall effect is of elaborate embellishment, bordering on the extravagant.

The most striking Lisbon buildings commissioned by Dom Manuel in the new style were the Monastery of Jerónimos at Belém and the nearby Tower of Belém.[19]

The site of the Hieronymite monastery had already been chosen for a chapel – the Ermida do Restelo – by Prince Henry the Navigator. Its association with maritime exploration was thus already established by the time Dom Manuel decided to erect an impressive monument to celebrate Vasco da Gama's great voyage. The work was put under the mastership of Diogo Boitac in 1502; he was succeeded by João de Castilho. But the most prominent sculptor to work at Belém was Nicolau Chanterene, the French artist who more than anyone else was influential in bringing the Renaissance style to Portuguese architecture. Although not much damaged by the 1755 earthquake, the monastery was clumsily restored in the nineteenth century, a fate shared by Pena chapel in Sintra. From its inception it was built to impress, as is recorded by a later French visitor to the city.

This monastery was commissioned by a Portuguese king, the very same in whose reign the Indies were discovered. No building could match its magnificence; the church in the shape of a cross is grandiose, and neither marble, nor gold, nor rich paintings were spared in its construction. The friars are lodged in a comfortable fashion that could be considered excessive.[20]

The most elaborate part of the building is the south portal, the work of João de Castilho. The façade is covered with statues crowned by a niche bearing the cross of the Order of the Kings of Christ. Prince Henry himself stares out from the central pillar. Two large windows are found to either side and there is an elaborate roof balustrade. The relief shows scenes from the life of St Jerome. Dom Manuel himself and his second wife, Dona Maria, are found on the west portal, which is somewhat blocked in by the connection of bridges to the more modern part of the building.

Some of the richest architectural features are to be found in the interior courtyard and cloisters. Carved stonework and network vaulting are particularly striking. The spiral decoration, niches and pillars are by Castilho, whilst the transepts, in High Renaissance style, are by Jeróme de Rouen, another Frenchman working in the royal service. King Manuel's tomb is in the chancel, in a classical style. The cloister is the most richly and elaborately decorated part of the monastery. The two-level galleries surround a square, each side measuring some 55 metres. The ground-level galleries have groined vaulting; wide arches with tracery rest on slender columns. Gothic and Renaissance styles are mingled; the first floor by Castilho is more delicate.

In contrast to the filigree exuberance of Jerónimos is the robustly square Tower of Belém nearby, now on the land's edge but originally right in the sea, built by Francisco de Arruda but embellished with what Fernando Pessoa called 'beautiful lacework'.[21] The tower was conceived as part of the monastery complex, acting as first line of defence for both the monastery and Lisbon harbour. It was completed in 1521 and dedicated to St Vincent, patron of the city.

Its bastion-like appearance (reflecting its defensive function) is softened by the balconies or loggias adorning the façade. The design shows some sophistication in the balancing of the circular casement sentry boxes (capped by domes, which add an exotic, Moorish feel to the building) with the open windows in the walls and the turrets, visible from every angle of vision. Richly carved niches, one facing seaward and dedicated to the Virgin, mark the façade. The external columns are topped with armillary spheres and magazines and store rooms remind us again of the defensive function of the tower and its symbol as an emblem of power and authority. An oratory links that military function to the religious quest to conquer Islam, ironic in the light of its florid, oriental touches, which include an echo of the shape of the hulls of caravels that were anchored in the river. Knotted hawsers and decorative cables add to the maritime effect of this example of high Manueline style. The writer Aquilino Ribeiro called it a 'stone ship' which told travellers they had reached the shores of Europe.[22] More than any other building, the tower is a symbol of Lisbon's connection with and command of the sea.

At Sintra, the king turned his attention to the royal palace, founded by King João I on the very site of the *walis* or Moorish governor's residence in the heart of the old village. A long scholarly dispute has raged over the ages about the authenticity of the Moorish features of the palace.[23] Although there is little doubt that King João built the palace on the site of a previous residence, the extent to which any remaining Moorish part of the building was absorbed into the new palace has never been authentically established. At any rate, what is clear from expert attention to details of the building and, especially, its ceilings is that Moorish methods of construction were used.[24] It is likely that this work was undertaken by *Mudejar* workmen – that is, from Moors who stayed to live under the Christian kings of Portugal and who were often confined to artisanal work. Ornate wooden ceilings, structures added at a much later period, were still executed according to Arabic techniques. Dom Manuel added an entire wing to the palace on the eastern side, fitting both the needs of his expanded family and containing salons and galleries worthy of his imperial pretensions. The works began in 1508 and detailed costs were kept by the builder, one André Gonçalves. The first distinctly Manueline feature is the decorative archway of the carriage entry which runs between Don Manuel's additions and the older parts of the palace. Arched internal doorways within follow the Moorish style.

On the façade of the new wing are six windows, three on each floor, overlooking the entrance court. The windows are all broadly similar in design, though details of decoration vary on each. Their Manueline features are immediately visible, which include fine frames in twisted, ornate form, but the windows also exhibit clear links with the earlier Moorish-style windows in the older western block. Each of the Manueline windows has two round-headed lights and a framing stand on corbelled-out bases at the side. The capitals are formed of wreaths of twisted foliage; on the lower floor one has twisted around it two branches, out of which grow the cusps. Decorative flowers are found engraved on them, sometimes in square shapes, sometimes round. Branches also intertwine on the sides, supporting three dramatic finials, capped with turban-shaped tops. While distinct in their exuberant naturalistic and exotic additions, the windows nevertheless have the same shape as the earlier Moorish ones and do not feel out of place when viewed with them.[25]

There are many Manueline features in this part of the building. A number of doorways are in the florid style; at the end of a passage, a doorway has a half-octagonal head with curved sides. The door leading into the Sala dos Cisnes is also Manueline. Inside other rooms, such as the Sala das Duas Irmãs (the Hall of Two Sisters), there is evidence that the older structure was embellished at the time of Dom Manuel. Two rows of columns and arches have been inserted below the ceiling. The arches are rounded and lack mouldings; the thin supporting columns are also round with eight-sided bases. The great hall of the Sala dos Brasões was completed at the end of King Manuel's reign.[26]

Portugal's imperial role depended upon a highly centralized administration based upon the personal direction of the crown. Both King João II and Dom Manuel ruled as absolutist monarchs, personally controlling the affairs of state through coteries of trusted advisers. These coteries, which could be drawn from the lower nobility or even the burgher classes, owed their position entirely to royal favour. Privileges granted to them by the crown included the lordship of manors and estates, in some cases exemption from certain taxes or rights to hunt or produce specified goods for the expanding court. The military orders (Knights Templar and Hospitaller) were bound to provide service to the crown, particularly in the defence of Lisbon and other important civic centres. Much of the regulation of affairs of state – the famous ordinances which Dom Manuel revised – was directed to commercial affairs, ensuring that the crown's source of wealth was duly protected. Foreigners, like the Italian merchants, were accorded important rights and given due recognition at court. Until the time of the Inquisition, the Jews too were respected for their part in the wealth-creating culture of the great seaport of Lisbon. These foreign communities played an essential part in a country which simply did not have a middle class of sufficient number (in contrast to the Italian city-states like Venice and Genoa or Holland) to sustain the businesses of a flourishing Lisbon.[27]

The most important and well-known account of Lisbon during the mid-sixteenth century is given in the chronicle of Damião de Góis.[28] Góis was a historian who had also seen diplomatic service in different parts of Europe. He had studied at the University of Louvain where he met Erasmus in 1512. Góis was an adherent of the new humanism that was the prevailing intellectual climate of the European centres of learning and that would underpin the scientific and philosophical advances of the early modern period. After his diplomatic career, Góis returned to Lisbon, with his Dutch wife, and settled down in a house near the castle. He was appointed to the job of Royal Historian at the Torre do Tombo, eventually institutionalized into the national archives. However, his last years were not to be tranquil. Long suspected of heresy, he was hauled before the Inquisition, convicted and imprisoned in Batalha. He died a few years later in suspicious circumstances, possibly a murder victim.

Góis makes clear from the start of his description that he is out to justify the description of Lisbon as 'Queen of the Seas', principally because of its worldwide connections with the opening up of the West African trade and the discovery of India.[29] A respectful classicist, he delves into the history of the name of the city as it was used by Varro, Asclepiades Mirlianus, Strabo and Pliny the Elder. Following André de Resende's lead, he declares 'Olisiponem' as the correct Latin spelling of Lisbon and accepts the legend linking the city's foundation to Ulysses.[30]

Nor is Góis wary of considering other local legends – like that of the Triton who inhabited a cave at the foot of the steep cliffs near the Cabo da Roca. Fuelling stories of this kind was a useful prelude to establishing Lisbon as a mythical as well as a real place; a city of symbolic glory which would match its commercial greatness. After setting out the various legends, he takes his reader on a tour of the city, noting all the important buildings in and around the city walls.

Although Góis's account is hyperbolic and he is overboastful about Lisbon's monuments in comparison with those of other European cities, we learn a great deal from him about churches, public buildings and the extent of the city's spread. His account confirms that by the sixteenth century the centre of gravity had irreversibly moved down from the heights of the medieval city to the riverside at the Terreiro do Paço. This huge open space, opening towards the sea, signifies a new stage in the urban psychology of the city. From the central square, the expansion of the city was in a westward direction, through Santos towards Belém. Along this stretch of coast suburban villas of 'admirable elegance and delight'[31] are sprinkled along the coast. They could be seen from the festively decorated royal barges that occasionally sailed along the coast, crammed with courtiers in glittering dress, entertained by musicians. Further out is the hermitage of São Julião (at Carcavelos) and the fort at Cascais.

The inner city area is still full of orchards and gardens; springs and running water can be found everywhere. Many buildings retain interior open spaces in the Moorish style. Góis singles out several 'sumptuous'[32] buildings for special mention. They are almost all façades of empire – the Public Granary, the New Customs House, the Ceuta and India Houses and the War Armoury. The Public Granary contains two wings with numerous internal arched galleries. It can be regarded as the granary of the nation and the 'pantry of Lusitania'.[33] The New Customs House is a magnificent building which extends right to the edge of the river. On the shore side it has an ornately decorated colonnade. Its great central courtyard bustles with markets of every description from those selling fish to others with sweets and rare spices, all showing up the spending power of the city dwellers. The India House nearby may justly be described as an opulent emporium, crammed as it is with aromas, precious stones, silver and gold. The War Armoury has numerous parts to it; its walls are adorned with fine art. This labyrinth is crammed full of weaponry, including 40,000 suits of armour for the infantry and 3000 pieces of cavalry gear. All these buildings reflect the imperial power that Portugal has become and the opulence that its overseas enterprise has brought to the capital.[34]

A less flowery account of Lisbon was published in the same year by Cristovão Rodrigues de Oliveira. He has a penchant for statistics, recording the fact that the city had 80,000 inhabitants, 432 streets, 89 alleys and 62 built-up complexes. He observes that sometimes development depended upon the sale of strategic sites by particular landlords. An example was in the Bairro Alto where the astrologer and surgeon Guedelha Palanciano owned much of the land. But Oliveira records five streets crossing in a north–south direction, even in this confined area.[35] Nor did this teeming city lack its social problems. Deaths from killing were a frequent occurrence, as they were in many other contemporary European cities; criminals were condemned to a frightful life at prisons such as the Galé prison, described later by Charles Dellon.

> This earth-bound *Galé* is built on the banks of the river and consists of two large apartments, one above the other. Both are full; the condemned sleep on benches covered with blankets. Their hair is cut and they are given a shave once a month. They wear workers' blouses and a cap made of blue cloth. They are also given a coat made of black serge wore for warmth during the day and used as a blanket at night.[36]

The prisoners' plight has, of course, to be seen in context of a low standard of living for most citizens. Cramped accommodation, lack of hygiene and decaying infrastructure all combined to make life unpleasant for the lower classes. Sometimes it was their sheer poverty that led to a lack of utilities. A visiting Frenchman records at a later date:

> They [the Lisbonites] have an awful way of sleeping. They lie down naked with no shirts, men and women, girls and boys in the same room. At night, because they don't have any beds they spread blankets and sheets on the floor, as many as necessary for the people present, and in the morning they put it all away, folding the blankets and sheets in a small room and the house is in order. At noon, they do the same thing for the siesta.[37]

During these years, the two Iberian nation-states of Portugal and Castile were being drawn closer together by dynastic ties. King Manuel himself had married three times to Spanish princesses. King João III, his son, married into the family of Emperor Charles V. Despite the tenacious independence fostered by the early Afonsin monarchs, these alliances encouraged the movement towards integration of the two major Iberian kingdoms. At the court, if not in the countryside, a cultural cosmopolitism also contributed to the unifying trend. Both Iberian languages were spoken by the upper classes; dynastic connections between aristocratic houses crossed the borders. It was also the case that common interests brought the

two nations together. After the settlements in the Atlantic on the
one hand (Treaty of Tordesillas, 1494) and in the East Indies on
the other (Treaty of Saragosa, 1529) the overseas rivalry between
Spain and Portugal ceased to be significant. Instead a common
stance against increasing pressure from other European maritime
nations – Holland, France and England created a need for mutual
defence. The Reformation and the accompanying Inquisition added
to a common cultural identity. In 1580 Filipe II, the son of Emperor
Charles, succeeded to the throne of Portugal and a united kingdom
was established.

The earlier cosmopolitanism of the court was even more evident
during the Spanish or Filipan period, as it is known. Figures like
the diplomat and writer Francisco de Melo (1608-1666), bilingual
and well known in Spain, became pivotal players. Eulogies of the
city, such as that of Luís Mendes de Vasconcelos, continued to be
published.[38] Mendes de Vasconcelos was a soldier and diplomat
of the new cosmopolitan breed and he encouraged the Spanish
king to consider the idea of moving the capital to Lisbon on the
grounds of its strategic position in terms of trade with the New
World. His vision was never realized. At the same time aristocratic
residences began to spill out of the central area towards Benfica in
the west and Campo Pequeno in the north. Over the whole period
the number of religious institutions continued to grow, from 21 at
the beginning to over 87 by the early eighteenth century. Lisbon
was admired by many Spanish visitors, including the dramatist
Molina, who rated it among the wonders of the world.[39] Nevertheless, a sense of the distinct nature of the Portuguese nation
never completely faded. The Portuguese monarchy was restored
in 1640 under the House of Bragança. After the restoration of the
Portuguese monarchy, buildings became even more sumptuous,
although the old, medieval lines of the streets remained largely
intact. It is in the panoramas of the city from the river that we see
it in its full, architectural splendour.[40]

3

The Holy City

From the very earliest times, men took to worshipping the gods along the banks of the Tagus estuary and at the windswept lands end to the west of Lisbon at the Cabo da Roca. The setting of the coast in particular – bounded by the mountain or *serra* of Sintra on the one side and the wild, craggy cliffs of the ocean on the other – could hardly fail to turn men's minds towards mortality and the role of the gods in their lives. Here in a naturally rugged setting, surrounded by the elements of water and wind and sun, with sudden sea mists covering the upland, prehistoric man was already building tributes to the gods in the form of dolmens and cromlechs and other funerary monuments.

At the rocky land's end – the *promunturium magnum* – man built his first temple, a shrine to the Goddess of the Moon, whose name became associated with Sintra, the *Mons Lunae* or Sacred Mount. Arches made up of stones, dating from prehistoric times, were set out in patterns reminiscent of those found throughout the ancient world from the Indian subcontinent to the Greek islands. The Goddess of the Moon and the Earth Goddess were at the centre of a cult which represented womanhood and, above all, fertility as the prime object of worship. Cybele, originally an Asiatic goddess, was transferred into Roman religion via the Greeks, whose name for her was Rhea, hardly distinguishable from earth itself.[1] Stone temples erected to the goddess were to be found on many sites in mainland Greece and scattered in the Aegean Islands. At the permanent stone temple on the rocky Sintra Cape, the priests and their acolytes worshipped Kinthia or Cynthia, the Greek Artemis or Roman Diana who was the Goddess of the Moon. From Cynthia came the place name Chentra and finally Cintra, the centre of the cult dedicated to her. The interest in lunar observation was linked to attention to solar eclipses. Sun and moon formed a duality in the old eschatology, represented in the difference of sexes too (Apollo was God of the Sun; Artemis Goddess of the Moon). Whilst Apollo represented the masculine qualities of energy and virility, his sister Artemis matched them with artistic, feminine characteristics. The early Iberians believed that this duality in the divine order was reflected in a balance of qualities in the earthly existence. It was important in devising religious rituals to pay due attention to these differing characteristics. The Celts, who followed the Iberians, also looked for harmonious patterns in a universe that would be otherwise unacceptably random in its operation.[2]

Evidence of religious worship in Neolithic times takes various forms. Curious, elongated inscriptions, some in the shape of diamond crosses, others in circles or spirals, have been uncovered on rock surfaces in the Colares valley and across the Lisbon area. They suggest no obvious utilitarian use but are rather a form of ancient hieroglyphics associated with solar and lunar cults. Other evidence is in more massive form – stone structures of various shapes and sizes from the period are scattered across the Lisbon area. Blocks of stone, in the form of a tabular slab, were placed on two supporting columns with an entrance space carved out below. These structures, or dolmens, like others found in other parts of Western Europe, were mausoleums where the dead were laid out to rest with proper respect to the gods. Each soul was allotted his own tumulus; rites of burial were carefully observed so that the dead person did not return to haunt the living. Within the tomb, the dead person was surrounded by his worldly possessions, indicating a belief in the continuity of the conditions of life in the afterlife.

These early prehistoric temples (and the Celtic structures that followed them) survived into the Roman era; in some cases they were incorporated into new buildings erected on top of them. The physical integration of different religious sites was matched by a fusion of cultural practices. Pagan cults were integrated with Roman worship and later found their way into Christian observances. In other cases, such as the rites surrounding the *lagarto da penha* (stone lizard associated with the cobra), they continued to have a distinctive life of their own.

The first large buildings dedicated to religious purposes were erected in Roman times. References are made to at least three major temples in Lisbon, namely those dedicated to Jupiter and to the goddesses Diana and Cybele. However, physical evidence in the form of remains has been scarce so that nothing has been found to indicate the extent of the temple either of Jupiter or of Diana, the latter believed to have been situated near São Jorge Castle. Remains of the temple of Cybele, although claimed to be of 'grand and magnificent structure'[3] consisted of a few broken columns, capitals and scattered stones found at the time of the earthquake of 1755. It is likely that worship of the 'Great Mother of the Gods' was brought by Phoenician and Greek sailors to Lisbon some time after the cult was first established in Asia Minor in the sixth century BC. Once she had been incorporated into the Roman panoply of gods and goddesses in consequence of a Sibylline prophecy in 204 BC, shrines to her would have been built all over the Roman world, including the one at Olisipo. But, in the absence of remains, we can only guess at the extent or grandeur of decoration that such a building would have had. More evidence, in the form of funerary monuments, has survived

from Roman cemeteries, which were scattered in the north and
north-east outskirts of the city.

A similar dearth of evidence lends sketchiness to our knowledge of the growth of Christianity in the Roman and early Suevic
periods. By the time of the Council of Nicaea in 325 AD the Church
was established enough to be represented by Bishop Potâmio.
Sometimes the mixing in of pagan superstitions had harmful
results. In 387 Bishop Priciliano, who was suspected of witchcraft,
was executed as a heretic. His death conferred a kind of instant
martyrdom for it led to the establishment of a cult which favoured
a more worldly, less monastic and inward-looking form of Christianity. Throughout the Suevic period the Church remained a
powerful political force, particularly after the conversion of King
Theodimir in 550 and the installation of St Martin as Archbishop
of Braga.[4]

St Martin's vision was of a secular state, Roman in structure
and Catholic in religion. The Christianity he preached would be
tolerant of pagan features in its ritual so that a rich cultural mix of
ancient Iberian, Roman and Christian elements would be created
from the fusion. The authority of the Church was confirmed by
the holding of councils at Braga in 563 and 572. They resulted in
a strengthening of the Church's internal organization, which in
turn made its grip on political life even stronger. The episcopal
base for this new order was in the diocese of Ossonoba, in the old
Roman province of Lusitania. There are few physical remains from
this period in the Lisbon area – only some Visigothic slabs and
stonework which do not compare with churches in other parts of
the country, for example that of Santo Amaro in Beja, with its
basilica-shaped plan and unusual Visigothic capitals.

For over four centuries the principal religion of Portugal, as of
other parts of the Peninsula, was Islam. Mosques were built in all
the significant cities, including Lisbon, but little physical evidence
of them has survived. In fact the principal architectural heritage
from the Moorish period is in the form of castles – such as the

castle at Sintra – but even these buildings have been extensively restored. The most significant, lasting Moorish features have been found in the interior of Portuguese buildings – in particular in the form of ceramic tiles. Typically Moorish decorative features – for example in window frames or arches (the famous horseshoe shape was probably adopted from the Visigothic model) adorn many medieval buildings. Art historians have traced the evolution of these oriental styles into the high-blown Renaissance form of the Manueline. Nevertheless because that style was regarded as nationalistic (and the nation was Christian Portugal) there has been a certain resistance to acknowledging Moorish influence on Portuguese culture in general, which has only gradually changed in recent times. Thus the Sintra historian Francisco Costa, in discussing the origins of the old Royal Palace at Sintra, brushed aside any suggestion that it could be considered as, in any way, a Moorish building, though he acknowledged the romantic appeal of suggesting an exotic origin for it.[5]

The most significant examples of religious architecture are to be found in the next period when the Romanesque style was spreading across Europe, being brought to Portugal by the kings of its first dynasty, the Burgundian. In Portugal, as elsewhere in Iberia, the style was adopted to local needs, so that churches and monasteries took on a fortified look, often featuring castellated battlements such as at Sé, the Cathedral of Lisbon. Behind the stern façades were thick walls, designed to be impenetrable to marauding Muslim enemies of the new Christian kingdom of Portugal. A good example of solid Romanesque style is to be found at Coimbra where the cathedral (Sé) has a solid, fortified appearance. The church is shaped in a Latin cross; something severe lingers in the three-aisled interior, with the high nave divided into arcade and triforium, the arcade round-headed. Austerity is reflected in the window openings (of the west face) although, as in other buildings of the period, later additions (including Gothic flourishes) make it difficult to discern the original.

Early Christian churches in the Lisbon area also exhibit similar protective features, particularly towers and observation platforms from where the enemy could be seen from a distance. Churches in all the central parishes – of São Martinho, Madalena and São Bartolomeu – had towers. These features were preserved on the fronts of churches even in the Jewish quarter. The fortified appearance of its churches, though resulting from more recent and real experience of war, gave Lisbon the same look as many other medieval European cities. The buildings were meant to be siege-proof; they had plain exteriors; within there was a growing tendency to elaboration as the Gothic took grip. São Vicente da Fora (outside the boundaries of the city, as its name implies) exhibits typically Romanesque features. It is also planned on a central Latin cross with three-sided nave. The outside, with its tower and protected windows, gives a sturdy, impenetrable look. The nearby Convent of Santo Agostinho shared these defensive features – battlements, a bell tower and thick, protective walls. As time went on, embellishments, as well as changes in the social function of Lisbon churches, altered their appearance. In the Martires parish, for example, the original semi-rustic buildings of the hermitage continued right into the sixteenth century, when they were transformed by florid Manueline additions. Sometimes the sober exteriors survived and the donations of parishioners and patrons were lavished on interior decoration, always the strongest part of the Portuguese architectural heritage.

The Cathedral (Sé) was founded in 1160 on the site of a mosque, which, as we have seen, may itself have been built on the remains of a Roman temple. Legend rather than archaeological evidence is the basis for the claim that the cathedral was built on the exact site of the mosque; in any event the foundation of Sé was an act of immense symbolic significance, which Afonso Henriques, first king of the new nation, understood very well. Lisbon had just been captured from the Moors by a cosmopolitan force under his command, which had included English mercenaries. As part of their reward, Gilbert of Hastings was installed as the first Bishop of Lisbon and he remained in post for 19 years, overseeing the construction of the cathedral and the consolidation of the ecclesiastical organization of the Lisbon see and its parishes. The Anglo-Norman style of the exterior was due to the superintendence of Roberto and Bernardo, the two master builders who erected the solid flanking towers and the battlements in classical Romanesque mould.[6] To their original design many Gothic features were later added; after the destruction caused by the earthquake of 1755 the central arches were reconstructed: neoclassical and baroque features appeared in the interior.

Whilst the external appearance of Sé, with its two sturdy towers, retained the original fortified aspect of the building, these interior embellishments changed its feeling as a place of worship. As in Coimbra, the principal plan was in the shape of the Latin cross; three naves and rounded arches in the transept gave a less austere impression – the use of space was becoming richer and less primitive. Both human figures and geometric or floral decorations are found in various parts of the building, adding to the 'softening' of the original simplicity of style. The capitals of the pillars are sculptured and date from the seventeenth century. The early Gothic features, which began to appear toward the end of the long period of construction, are found principally in the north face of the exterior and inside along the interception of the transept and the doors. The cloisters and galleries were added in the reign of Dom Dinis (1279-1325); they too are Gothic in feel with ribbed arches giving a view of the central courtyard, reminiscent of the Monastery of Alcobaça. An overall balance is achieved by the two-tiered cloister, with sculptured capitals to the columns in Renaissance style.

At about the same time the chapel of São Bartolomeu, on the north side of the church, was built. Here the stonework is more elaborate; the ambulatory is cased in an ogival ceiling. The ceiling itself is supported by elaborate fenestration, in a florid Gothic style.

Replacements had to be made after an earthquake struck the city in 1344. Lowering of windows enabled light to be directed into the choir stands. After the earthquake of 1755, showy, baroque features, including gilt effects, were added to parts of the interior. Renovation work, undertaken in the twentieth century, was not always of the most sensitive type, sometimes overlaying originals with more elaborate finishes.

The early medieval aspect of Sé is captured in an *azulejo* panel now in the National Museum of Azulejos, at the Convent of Madre de Deus. The panel depicts the solid, west front towers, capped by small pointed belfries offering an almost oriental look. The bell tower to the rear lacks this refinement so that it seems a sturdy, background support to the whole building, keeping any ethereal tendency in check. By the side wall, soldiers are seen fending off Moorish attackers who use bows to shoot at the de-fenders and ladders to scale the castle-like walls. The tableau as a whole represents the various architectonic features of the cathedral and the changing role from the early days of being a Christian fortress.

An important symbol of the city, two black ravens, grew out of the association of St Vincent the Martyr with Sé cathedral. Vincent of Saragosa (who died in 304 AD at Valencia), as a result of the anti-Christian edicts of the emperors Diocletian and Maximilian, suffered a particularly gruesome death even by the standards of early Christian martyrdoms.[7] He was first weakened by enforced starvation. Then he was racked and roasted on a gridiron; finally he died in the stocks from the accumulated effects of these tortures. The relics of the saint were supposed to have been brought to Portugal in Moorish times. The relics remained hidden for some time in the south of the country until after the consecration of Sé Cathedral, when they were brought out from their hiding place and taken to Lisbon. The boat in which they came was escorted by a pair of black ravens. A cult of St Vincent immediately sprang into being; the saint was declared to be the patron saint of the city. At the same time the black ravens became a symbol of Lisbon and were incorporated into its coat of arms.[8]

Some 30 years after the foundation of the cathedral, in 1195, one Fernando de Bulhão (who was to succeed St Vincent as patron saint of the city) was born in a nearby palace and baptized in the cathedral itself. His father was Martinho de Bulhão, a courtier who had successively served Afonso Henriques and Dom Sancho, the first two kings of Portugal. The young boy proved to be intelligent and precocious, achieving high academic attainment in many subjects. He also showed a markedly religious bent, taking the name of Anthony when he joined the Order of Augustinian Canons in his early teens. He studied at Coimbra; in 1220 he joined the Franciscan brotherhood and sailed to Morocco. He had to return from North Africa due to ill health but took part in the General Chapter at Assisi in the following year. This meeting was presided over by Brother Elias; St Francis himself no longer acted as organizer of the Order. When not preaching, the Franciscan brothers retired to prayers or the performance of liturgy, leading a life of spartan simplicity. The buildings they lived in were modest abodes, their churches largely unadorned, with little or no furniture. Only gradually did the preaching brothers gain a reputation as theologians and begin to teach in the universities and seminaries. St Anthony, with his intellectual prowess, was one of the first to do so, lecturing at Bologna, Montpellier and Toulouse in turn.

However, it was his preaching that brought the young Franciscan fame. His charismatic presence, fine voice and bearing added authority to his sermons. The large crowds that gathered to hear him could not be accommodated inside churches, so that St Anthony took to speaking in market places where larger congregations could gather. His message was to emphasize the pristine simplicity of the life of Christ; avarice and usury were his regular targets. When he moved to Padua, he devoted almost all his time to preaching.

The cult of St Anthony developed apace after his death and nowhere more devotedly than in Lisbon, his home town. A profusion of miracles were associated with it; St Anthony himself was depicted preaching to fishes, guarding animals or teaching. A popular iconographical representation showed the saint with a book and lily and the infant Jesus in his arms. His devotion to the poor was particularly emphasized in charitable works ('St Anthony's bread') and his talents were said to extend to the finding of lost articles. A chapel was established across the road from the cathedral near to the site of his family home.

If Sé Cathedral straddled the boundaries of Romanesque and Gothic, there can be no doubt about the style of one of the city's most dramatic monuments – the ruins of the Convento do Carmo, high up on the slopes above the Chiado. The present elaborate folly, which also houses the Archeological Museum, was designed after the earthquake of 1755 as a partially restored, romantic ruin. Inspecting engravings before that time, for example in 1745, we can see a grand Gothic structure, rounded cloisters and massive west wing serving as a monastic centre of imposing proportions. Building began in 1389 on steeply sloping terrain, something that posed a considerable engineering challenge. Levelling and reinforced supporting structures were put in place by an army of stonemasons and labourers led by the Anes family. Heavy joints, on which the foundations rested, were first laid. The traditional, Latin-crossed structure took eight years to build, with naves and walls gradually emerging. Massing arches supported the great, arching roof. The Carmelite brothers, who were waiting to take up residence, were installed in the northern part where the ground was flatter.

By 1399 a gabled south portal, with its impressive arch and bearing the name of Master Builder Gomes Martins, was already in place, although further supports for the building had yet to be constructed. The overall plan, with similarities to that of Batalha Monastery, consisted of a principal east chapel, of dramatic height, flanked by four polygonal apses, two to each side. The transept itself consisted of three naves, the central one being the highest. Ornate, Gothic ogival crosses and arches decorate all the naves imposing a uniform style. Other decorative features – the rose window and fleur-de-lis on the stonework – were destroyed in the great earthquake. Over the generations radical changes were made to the fenestration. Gothic windows were fitted in the main nave; elaborate Manueline decorations of floral and vegetal design are found on the capital of columns. Some of these decorative features echo biblical iconographic themes, in some cases depicting an ethereal Jerusalem, in others the imposing Temple of Solomon.

From one balcony there were views down to Rossio Square, later the scene of ritual burning of heretics – the auto-da-fé – from the early sixteenth century. The restoration after the earthquake followed the taste of the time for fanciful ruins rather than any serious attempt at restoration of the original building. Nevertheless standing in the main nave with the open sky showing above the vaulted Gothic arches above is a dramatic experience, giving a graphic impression of the grandeur of the original building.[9] The presence of the Archaeological Museum is perhaps a symbol of the search for earlier, pre-Christian roots.

The Manueline extravagances which we have considered in the previous chapter were overtaken by a new Mannerist style in the sixteenth century. As we have seen, those Manueline projects were, on the whole, public as well as monumental undertakings; the building of the Mannerist period is more domestic in scale. Whilst the façades of the houses of the aristocracy going up in the Bairro Alto could be grand enough, the overall feeling was of urban domestic architecture which afforded plenty of opportunity to show off opulence within. Two of the principal churches to be built in this period were São Vincente da Fora, just outside the city walls, and the Jesuit establishment at São Roque. The main foreign influence during this period was the Italian – championed by Francisco de Holanda, who had spent much time in Italy in the company of Michelangelo himself.[10] The 'Mannerist' school derived its very name from the Italian word for style. In a departure from the medieval tradition of anonymity, the individual artist was now identified because his intellectual conviction and artistic sensibility were regarded as an important aspect of the process of creativity. The inner harmony of the artist was matched against the outward symmetry of nature. De Holanda advanced a neo-Platonic theory to link the mind of the artist to his work. Although his thought was original, there is nothing to suggest that de Holanda saw his new idealism as a break from Renaissance classicism. Italianate chapels were set up in several churches, including Nossa Senhora da Luz, as well as in São Roque itself.

São Vicente de Fora was one of the earliest Lisbon churches to be built after the Reconquest. Its founder was no less a personage than Afonso Henriques himself, who had ordered his English bishop, Gilbert of Hastings, to erect two churches in celebration of the return of Christianity to Portugal. The site of São Vicente da Fora was chosen to mark the spot where crusaders, many of them foreigners in the service of the Portuguese prince, had been killed in their attempts to storm the Moorish citadel. Another foreigner, the Flemish monk Brother Gualtero, was installed as Abbot. The church was dedicated to the martyr-saint Vincent, beginning a cult that became deeply rooted in the emerging Portuguese nation. As its adherents became more fanatical, they were accused of idolatry by those less committed. The poet Frei António das Chagas was to make ironic use of this notion, suggesting in his verse that one might enter the Church of São Vincente a true Catholic and emerge from it as an idolater.[11]

The original church was built in Romanesque style but like most buildings of its type was subject to many alterations and additions over the centuries. The major reconstruction took place during the reign of Filipe II, which began in 1598. The Spanish monarch had come to admire Lisbon and was even considering the possibility of making it the capital of his united Iberian kingdom.

He brought with him the Castilian royal architect Juan de Herrara, who had been involved in the building of the Escorial near Madrid. Although Herrara's name is on the plan, it is not clear how much part he played in the actual construction of the building. Balthazar Alvares is cited as the principal architect, with the interiors done by Pedro Nunes Tinoco or the Italian Filipe Terzi. The building went at a slow pace, only being completed fifty years later. That length of programme itself confirms the involvement of many hands.

São Vincente da Fora added majestically to the Lisbon skyline. Its dome, looming high on the hill, complemented that of the Ribeira Palace, built at about the same time, on the river's edge. The monastery symbolized a new mood of aggrandizement, though the belfry towers placed at ends of a elegant neoclassical façade, harked back to the earlier fortified tradition. Following the pattern of São Roque, the interior (where Balthazar Antunes also worked) featured a single, longitudinal knave with intercommunicating chapels, a style favoured by the Jesuits. Plain Doric columns give a severe effect, drawing attention to the elaborate Joanine high altar. The interior of the sacristy, where Tinoco worked, is more elaborate, with fine tiling and a painted wooden ceiling. The monastery housed an important collection of religious paintings which have subsequently found their way to the Museum of Ancient Art in Rua das Janelas Verdes on the slopes of Lapa. The prominence and grandeur of the building were recognized when the Patriarchal Church was moved there in the eighteenth century and the monks then in residence had to move to Mafra.

A decision had already been made in 1525 to build a church on the site of an ancient hermitage at São Roque. The outside façade of the present church is severe, joined in linear surfaces and visible some way down the hill on whose slopes it extends. The interior contains a compact single nave with an upper gallery running above the eight side chapels. These are placed symmetrically to the right and left of the main altar; small altars give on to the transept.

The main chapel, begun in the early seventeenth century, includes in the retable images of the four great saints of the Jesuit order – Ignatius Loyola, Francis Xavier, Luís de Gonzaga and Francisco de Borja. A statue of Our Lady of the Visitation occupies the lower central niche, the overall style of which is neoclassical. Groups of double Corinthian columns adorn it; the whole chapel is encased in a rounded arch which is set in severe plain columns on each side. This neoclassical motif is echoed in the chapel of St Francis Xavier (where the saint is seen being received by King João III prior to his departure for India) and the chapel of Santo António, later restored in the nineteenth century.

However, the architectural gem of the church is the chapel of St John the Baptist, which the king commissioned in Italy and which was brought to Portugal in 1742. The work was undertaken by Luigi Vanvitelli and Nicola Salvi and took almost a decade to construct. Although rocaille elements are evident in its decoration, the structure is quite severely neoclassical and gives the impression of perfect symmetry. Precious metals, including gilt bronze, and precious stones, such as lapis lazuli, agate, green porphyry, alabaster and jade, were used. The panels depict the Visitation, Pentecost and Baptism of Christ. Medallions and angels are wrought from Carrara marble. An exquisite balance and harmony are achieved in the design.

The glorification of God in magnificent churches in Lisbon testified to the immense material wealth of the Roman Catholic Church. From the very inception of the kingdom in the twelfth century, the Church had played a major role in the affairs of state. Once Portugal itself had been liberated from Moorish rule, religious attention turned to overseas. Expeditions to North Africa were regarded as crusades and had the full blessing of the Church; when exploration began along the African coast under Prince Henry the Navigator, the motive was as much to convert savages as it was to advance commerce. As the empire grew, priests such as the Jesuits in Brazil played a significant part in the expansion of the state's power. The Jesuit St Francis Xavier established himself in Goa and from there his proselytizing mission spread across the entire Far East.

At home the Church benefited by becoming the second largest property owner, only outmatched in extent of ownership by the crown itself. Throughout the early medieval period deeds relating to the setting up of religious orders and the granting of land to them abound. Under successive royal charters, the clergy gained more and more privileges, including a tenure of office that protected them even from royal interference. Religious institutions grew at such a pace that in 1220 an inquiry into the rights and privileges of the clergy was instituted by the king. Monasteries were founded at Chelas, at São Vincente de Fora and at Trindade, the latter placed on the higher slopes of the city.

During this early period the practice of religious tolerance, which had existed during most of the Moorish period, continued, although there was always pressure for Jews and Muslims to convert to Christianity. While there was no legal requirement for them to do so, social and cultural pressures resulted in discrimination for those who resisted conversion. Jews were debarred from certain occupations, including service to the crown, and forced into taking up commercial jobs, at which they proved very successful. Their ghettoes, the *judiarias*, were based around the old synagogues which had survived throughout the Muslim period and were conveniently close to the trading heart of the city. The *Mujadin* or Moors who stayed after the Reconquest were also banned from public office. Their influence was felt mainly in the area of architecture and arts and crafts, where as the principal workforce they continued to use traditional Mozarabic methods and decorative effects. However, towards the end of the fifteenth century this climate of tolerance was beginning to be eclipsed by a new fanaticism. Although King João II allowed free passage to Jews escaping persecution from Spain in 1496, his successor, Dom Manuel, first instituted forced conversions of 'New Christians'.

Dom Manuel's policy was guided by an ambition to become the leading monarch in Iberia. He had married into the Castilian royal family, which had already sanctioned the setting up of the Inquisition in Spain. The Church supported the mass conversion of Jews and Muslims; those who refused to convert were put on ships and sent off to North Africa, sometimes separated from their families. The 20,000 who remained accepted Christianity, although from the very start deep suspicion lingered that they were continuing to practise their own religion in secret. Incidents started to flare up between the communities, which up to that time had coexisted in peace. The Jews only felt safe in their own homes, although even there they could be spied on. A case recorded in the Sintra archive tells of how some Jews were followed through the streets by a child who crept behind them indoors and subsequently reported seeing a proscribed ceremony being performed. Although first convicted of a charge of profanity in the lower court, the Jews appealed and, remarkably, the verdict was quashed by a higher authority.[12]

Meanwhile in Lisbon itself things began to take a sinister turn. An epidemic of plague swept through the city in the autumn of 1505, prompting the departure of the king and the court from the capital. As food shortages added to the plight of the Lisbon populace, the situation deteriorated. Anger was directed towards the Jewish community in particular since it seemed the only group still enjoying a reasonable standard of living. More charges against them were trumped up; some were accused of denying miracles; others were found observing Passover.

Despite a royal intervention to try to protect the Jews, the situation was rapidly spiralling out of control. Dominican monks, who had remained in the beleaguered city, influenced the desperate rabble by inciting them to act against the infidels in their midst. Hundreds of Jews and Moors were rounded up in the streets – women and children as well as men – and physically abused. Meanwhile groups of young men roamed the city attacking anyone they came upon who could remotely be associated with the two minority communities. Brutal assaults turned into murder; bodies were dragged and dumped outside the Dominican monastery.[13]

This reign of terror lasted for about a week before the authorities, realizing that the city was slipping into anarchy, intervened decisively. The army was called in; troublemakers were rounded up and summarily executed; the Dominicans were arrested and several of them executed. Local councillors who had failed to act with authority had property confiscated. The title 'most noble and royal city' was rescinded. If Dom Manuel had persisted in this policy, matters might have returned to normal and the course of subsequent Portuguese history might have been very different. As it was, his wife, Queen Maria, would not allow a policy contrary to that of her Spanish relatives to be pursued in a land where she reigned as queen. She had the Dominicans reinstated and, far from drawing a veil over their activities, succeeded in getting the king to reverse his previous policy of protecting his minority subjects. Dom Manuel himself still harboured an ambition to reign over a united Iberian kingdom, and so to curry favour with the Castilian monarch he pursued the same anti-Semitic and anti-Moorish policies already in place across the border. Before long, a formal request was made to Rome for the establishment of the Inquisition in Portugal. A headquarters was found at the Palace of Estaus, near Rossio in the heart of the city. By 1536 the Inquisition, housed in some grandeur in Rossio Square, was, in Saramago's words, acting like a 'police force, a tribunal' that 'pursue, judge and sentence its enemies like any other tribunal or police force, sentence them to prison, exile and the stake'.[14]

Intellectuals, as always, were the targets for the zealots bent on persecution. In 1550 the Scotsman George Buchanan, who was installed as a teacher at Coimbra, was arrested together with a number of his colleagues. Buchanan had long been suspected of heterodoxy; a waverer of satirical bent and forthright intellect, he had been imprisoned in his native Scotland for staging what had been regarded as a heretical play before the king. During a later career in France his pronouncements on a number of issues, including free will, the Mass, prayers and religious garb, were regarded as suspect, even blasphemous.

The Lisbon Inquisitors raked up all of these matters from Buchanan's past, trying to build up a dossier that proved him a heretic. Buchanan put up a subtle defence when he was finally brought before the tribunal. While adopting a tone of repentance for past minor lapses, he showed by considerable theological dexterity the absurdity of the main charges against him. He also pointed to his exemplary life as a teacher at Coimbra where no hint of heterodox opinions had passed his lips. If proof were needed that he was an entirely reformed character, his career in Portugal showed it. The Inquisitors took their time. Buchanan was examined 18 times over a period of months; during his confinement he translated psalms into Latin. His *pièce de résistance* when accused of practising Judaism in his Scottish period was to point out that there were no Jews in Scotland and therefore it would have been literally impossible to practise that faith.

Sometimes the Inquisition enlisted foreigners to infiltrate communities suspected of deviance. Such a figure was an English Jesuit priest, Henry Floyd, who was in Portugal in the 1590s and early 1600s.[15] Floyd operated from the newly founded Residency. He had easy access to the English community, most of whom worked in the Factory or trading house. His object was to try to reconvert as many Englishmen as he could to Catholicism; his method was to pick on the most vulnerable, such as young bachelors who were homesick and lonely and glad to have a sympathetic fellow Englishman to guide them. His other victims were from the prison population, who were also easy targets for his sophistry. Personal charm and an extreme cunning brought Floyd much success and gained him admiration among the Society's superiors. His activities naturally attracted the suspicion of the English envoy, who already knew of Floyd's alleged association with the Gunpowder Plot. But it was difficult to act against a priest who had now got himself secured in the Jesuit stronghold of São Roque from where the leading Inquisitors were appointed.

Meanwhile new churches continued to be built in different parts of the city. One of the earliest Baroque churches to be built in Lisbon after the restoration of the Braganças in 1660 was Santa Engracia (also known as Nossa Senhora da Graça). Like many Lisbon churches it was built on the foundations of an old monastery, in this case an Augustinian one of the twelfth century. Work had actually started in 1632 but it seems that for half a century no major additions were made until João Antunes appeared as master mason. There seems to be some doubt about his previous experience since he is not associated with other major projects, but he took his commission seriously, producing a detailed plan in a matter of months.[16] What is clear is his familiarity with Italian styles and motifs – the coloured marble and twisted columns of the church attest to that taste. The building was conceived in the shape of a Greek cross, bordered by four solid towers. This plan, which was bold in conception, nevertheless retained a traditional Portuguese penchant for the robust, showing what a clever adaptation Antunes could make of the Italian style. Large pilasters in Tuscan mould adorn the outside, divided into two levels with a balcony running around the entire length of the building at the level of intersection. The main portal shows most sign of Baroque ornamentation, with twisted supporting columns, scrolled mouldings and an elaborate representation of the royal coat of arms, adorned by putti. The interior of the church is open and grand, with 34 pilasters, supporting sweeping arches in a semi-circular pattern. They lead up to the high altar, which is capped by a heavenly arch. The harmonious balancing of chapels, arches and central space is singularly impressive. Light falling on the polychromal stone at various angles adds to the unusual effect of the curving walls.

Extraordinary in its architectural design, Santa Engrácia does not share the lavish *talha dourada* interior of other Baroque churches of the city. The developing passion of embellishing wood with gilding could still be combined with Mannerist features – such as at the Igreja dos Anjos – but gradually the national style became more ornate and elaborate. Antunes himself contributed significantly to its development, for example at the Convento of Nossa Senhora da Conceição dos Cardais where twisted gilded columns encircle the entire retable in an arch and Dutch tiles are incorporated into the decorative features.

In the typology of Baroque churches we can identify those where the rich gilded effect predominates, others where the azulejo tiles play a more prominent role and finally those in which there is a combination. In the latter case, examples of which can be seen at Madre de Deus, the blue and white tiles, depicting land-scape scenes, are used to soften the overwhelming richness of the woodwork. In some cases, for example at the Igreja Paroquial das Mercês, the architect, in this case António de Oliveira Bernardes, has also embellished a ceiling in the azulejo style. As Portuguese Baroque developed it assimilated many different influences, most notably oriental motifs and patterns. Additional flourishes were provided when the style was taken abroad. In the Minais Gerais province of Brazil, Antonio Francisco Lisboa (known as 'O Alei-jadinho') designed elaborate doorways and windows.[17]

In the early eighteenth century the wealth pouring in from Brazil in the form of gold and diamonds was having a significant effect on all the Portuguese architectural and decorative arts. King João V 'The Munificent' undertook a series of lavish projects, not all of which were ecclesiastical.[18] A new aqueduct was built to service Lisbon; at Coimbra the king supported the extravagant new library; while at Evora the new Jesuit academy also received royal patron-age. But the king's most lavish monument was at Mafra, north of Sintra, where he built a large new palace complex that included a fine domed, marble church in the Italian neoclassical style. In the long wings of the main façade were spacious royal apartments, towards the rear extended cloisters, gardens and courtyards form-ing the monastery. The building of Mafra started in 1717, under the supervision of João Ludovice,[19] a German architect, after the birth of an heir to the throne, and continued for the remainder of the king's reign. As many as 30,000 craftsmen, drawn from all over the country, were involved in working at Mafra. Towards the end of his long reign the king embarked upon another great project at Queluz, just to the west of Lisbon, where a palace modelled on Versailles was to take over from Sintra Palace as the out-of-town residence of the royal family.[20] The architect there was the Portuguese Mateus Vicente de Oliveira. He was assisted in much of the design and in the layout of the elaborate, formalized gardens by Jean-Baptiste Robillon, a versatile Frenchman who had been in the service of Thomas Germain, silversmith and supplier to the Portuguese court.[21]

King João's most dramatic success in supporting the Church came early in his reign when he answered the pope's appeal for help to prevent Turkish expansion in the Adriatic. The Portuguese navy was dispatched to the Church's assistance and it won a significant victory at the Battle of Matapan in 1717. For this act of support the king was given the title of the 'Most Faithful' and the archepiscopacy of Lisbon was elevated to a patriarchate. Crown and Church acted in close unison, something only interrupted during Pombal's dictatorship after the earthquake of 1755.

Pombal's reforming programme, which included a separation of Church and State, was put aside once he fell from power. In 1777 Queen Maria ascended to the throne and immediately began to reinstate the clergy in positions of influence in the court. She also commissioned the large church near the fashionable area of Buenos Ayres, despite the fact that a large part of the city had still not been rebuilt. William Beckford, arriving in 1787, stayed in a house made of wood, and the royal palace itself at Ajuda was also still a wooden structure. The queen was a devotee of the cult of the Sacred Heart of Jesus – the new church (Estrela) was to be its centre. She chose as architect Mateus Vicente de Oliveira, who had been involved in work at Mafra under the direction of the great Ludovice.

Oliveira chose to build in the neoclassical style, echoing something of the majestic façade of Mafra in the new church. This consisted of a portico and Corinthian columns with matching belfry towers. A large cupola added to the Italian appearance of the building. Inside the church the architect maintained a certain austerity. Marble was used extensively with niches for statues in the Roman style. Towards the high altar, placed under the arching dome, green and blue marble pilasters are used to lighten the overall effect. Pompeo Batoni's painting for the high altar contains the theme of the Sacred Heart.

Under Maria and her immediate successor, João VI, the Church continued to remain a large property holder and a force to be reckoned with in national affairs. But during the radical upheavals of the early nineteenth century, when the absolutist nature of the monarchy was challenged, the Church was no longer protected to the same degree. After the civil war, which lasted from 1828 to 1834, the constitutionalists held sway and their anti-clericalism could no longer be held in check by a weakened monarchy. In 1834 the religious orders were abolished; church property was sold off by the government to boost a faltering economy. It is estimated that there were as many as 380 monasteries and 130 convents in the whole country but with many of them located in the Lisbon area. These were appropriated for public use at many levels. Parliament itself was housed in the Convent of São Bento da Saude, where it has remained;[22] the military took over the convents of Carmo, Graça and Mafra, the police seized Trinas de Mocambo; hospitals and schools were set up in others. The National library was located in the Convent of São Francisco. Although the architectural surroundings of these public offices could be grand, reflecting the past magnificence of the Church, the interiors were often ill suited to the purposes of the institutions that had moved into them. That disfunctionality added to demoralization in the public service, which would have depressed Pombal the reformer.

Emblem of the City of Lisbon (showing ravens,
the mythical guardians of St Vincent, patron saint of the city).

Jerónimos Monastery.
Engraving by W. Barclay, nineteenth century.

Interrogation by the Tribunal of the Inquisition.
Engraving, unknown, 1808.

Execution of those Condemned by the Tribunal of the Inquisition.
Engraving, unknown, 1722.

Perspective of Lisbon.
Print by G. Braunio, sixteenth century.

Ribeira Palace.
Engraving, unknown, nineteenth century.

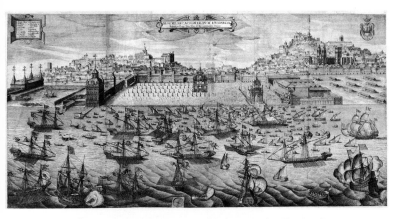

Embarcation of Catherine of Bragança for England.
Engraving, unknown, seventeenth century.

Triste Tableau des effets causés par le Tremblement de Terre.
Engraving, unknown, eighteenth century.

Dom Fernando de Saxe-Coburg Gotha.
Lithograph, *c.* 1850.

António Feliciano de Castilho, 1859.

Rua Augusta
by Alex Michellis, 1842.

Alexandre Herculano
by Alberto, *c.* 1870.

The Church was never to recover its sphere of influence. Anticlericalism remained rife during the First Republic, which began in 1911. Only in the later stages of the Salazar period, when the dictator had found it convenient to have the backing of the Church for his nationalistic policies, especially overseas, did it in any way regain political influence. But its physical and psychological mark upon the city of Lisbon had long been made and endures to the present day.

Earthquake City

The churches and other ecclesiastical buildings of Lisbon, which we have considered in the previous chapter, were concentrated in a dense area of building in the city centre. The grand Patriarchal complex, with its sumptuous church, was the most impressive of these conglomerations, but up the slope from it was the Jesuit church of São Roque with its fine chapels, whilst nearby Rossio square contained both the Convent of São Domingues and the Palace of the Inquisition (on the site of the present National Theatre of Dona Maria II). To the west was São Paulo in hilly Santa Catarina.[1] Numerous convents and monasteries, such as São Vicente da Fora, stretched out to the east just outside the old centre. A majority of the forty or so parish churches were also in the central area.

Intermingled with the churches and convents were grand public buildings such as the Customs House and the colonial trading agencies, which we have seen were built in the reign of Dom Manuel. The Paço da Ribeira, the royal palace, stood in the Terreiro do Paço or central square on the river's edge. It was crammed with stately furniture, tapestries and rare *objets d'art*, particularly of oriental origin. Indian furniture was mingled with Chinese ceramics, as befitted the imperial pretensions of Manueline Portugal. Other public buildings, such as the Casa da India, were built on a grand scale, with numerous wings and internal courtyards. They were decorated in ornate styles, reflecting the newly acquired imperial aspirations of the nation. A large complex of these buildings inter-linked to the royal palace, physically uniting the administrative and commercial features of empire. The colonial contribution to Lisbon was substantial, as borne out in an observation about Lisbon harbour made by a Frenchman in 1699.

> During my stay in Lisbon, the fleets from Angola, Brazil and the Indies arrived. There were ninety ships of which fifty-four had Lisbon as their final destination and thirty-six were headed to Porto. I went out to see this armada in a canoe and found myself caught in the middle of the firing canons that jumped repeatedly. All the ships brought home rich cargoes and it was rumoured that the ship from the Indies brought goods worth sixteen million.[2]

To this Manueline city, King João V, who reigned from 1706 to 1750, had added further ornate buildings in the prosperous years in the half-century before the earthquake. He totally redesigned and enlarged the old royal palace. The building works at the palace went on for years under the supervision of Ludwig, architect of Mafra, as we have seen in the previous chapter.[3] If the royal col-lection had always shown an inclination to the exotic and Eastern, King João wanted to create a setting of grandeur in which to show it off. Heavily gilded, Baroque features were created in the interiors; rare and valuable tapestries were hung; furniture was covered in fine brocades. Collections of works of art were purchased at home and abroad: a number of works by Rubens passed into royal hands in the 1720s; impressive architectural models of palaces and churches of Rome were acquired at the same time. Throughout his reign the bibliophile monarch went on amassing his library. His agents scoured European markets in search of the latest scientific literature as well as rare manuscripts and engravings.[4]

Meanwhile the spendthrift king lavished attention and funds on the building of the Patriarchal Church, with its adjoining palace, on a scale that he hoped would rival the Vatican and put Lisbon on a footing with Rome. Other palaces in the area, the homes of the court aristocracy, were also sumptuous. Dom Luis de Sousa had amassed a library of 30,000 volumes displayed in four Italianate rooms with lavish gilded *stucchi* in his house near the cathedral. The Conde de Vidigueira, who had been ambassador at the French court and who no doubt had been impressed by its regal grandeur, arranged another imposing library in spacious rooms, decorated with Italian paintings and statues, near São Roque Church.[5] Important collections of art, rare libraries and masses of gold and silverware were scattered in other aristocratic houses in the central area.

As Masses began on the fateful morning of 1 November 1755, in the midst of these splendours in what had become one of the most ornate cities in Europe, no one could have guessed at what the events of the day would bring. The scene that fine autumn morning is vividly set in a letter from an anonymous English witness.

> There was never a finer morning than the First of November, the sun shone out in its full lustre, the whole face of the sky was perfectly serene and clear, and not the least signal nor warning of that approaching event, which has made this once flourishing, opulent and populous city, a scene of the utmost horror and desolation except only such as served to alarm, but scarce left a moments time to fly from the general destruction.[6]

The first tremor was felt after 9.30 in the morning. It took the form of a loud and sinister rumbling noise that shook buildings but did not cause immediate damage. The English correspondent records that the sound was like that of thunder and that it lasted for less than a minute.[7] It was followed by two more violent quakes which were of sufficient strength to bring down roofs, walls and, in some cases, entire buildings. Much of the central and western parts of the city was affected. The English eyewitness, staying in

Buenos Ayres (modern Lapa), slightly to the west of the old centre, describes the moment of impact:

> The house I was in shook with such violence that the upper stories immediately fell and though my apartment, which was on the first floor, did not then share the same fate, yet was everything thrown out of its place, in such sort that 'twas with no small difficulty I kept on my feet and expected nothing less than to be soon crushed to death as the walls continued rocking to and fro, in the frightfullest manner; opening in several places; large stones falling down from every side from the cracks and the ends of most of the rafters starting out from the roof.[8]

When the shaking had stopped, a suffocating cloud of dust enveloped the whole city, choking the panic-stricken inhabitants who were crawling about in the debris. In this confusion the English eyewitness attempted to make his way down towards the river to escape by water. However, he found the entire street piled high with debris. Instead he turned eastwards towards São Paulo Church, which he found in ruins. The great church had collapsed into a pile of rubble after the second tremor, killing a large number of the congregation and others who had rushed into the building for safety. The streets in the whole central area running from São Paulo Church to the Royal Palace were the most severely affected, with buildings reduced to complete ruins or standing semi-derelict with only the odd wall intact. There were scenes of chaos everywhere. The eyewitness reports seeing priests still clad in their vestments from celebrating Mass, women half-dressed and without shoes, screaming children and terrified animals jostling to escape.

A similar account of the horrors was recorded by Thomas Chase, a young member of the British Factory, who fell from the fourth floor of his house but managed to survive in the debris in the basement with a broken arm and bruises. First sheltering in the burnt-out ruins of the Royal Palace, he eventually managed to escape by river to an English merchant ship moored on the Tagus.

Chase describes the stench, and the corpses burning in the flames,
the devotion of the parish priests who tried to console their flocks,
and the rapacious boatmen who could not resist cashing in on the
situation. But this was not the end of the misery; nor had the horror
ended. Our first eyewitness commentary continues:

> On a sudden I heard a general outcry. The sea is coming in, we shall
> all be lost. Upon this, turning my eyes toward the river, which at that
> place is near four miles broad I could perceive it heaving and swelling
> in a most unaccountable manner, as no wind was stirring. In an instant
> there appeared at some small distance a vast body of water, rising, as
> it were like a mountain, came on foaming and roaring, and rushed
> towards the shore with such impetuosity that tho' we all immediately
> ran for our lives, many were swept away.[9]

This was the first of a series of seismic waves that hit the
Lisbon–Cascais coast about two hours after the original tremors.
Coming from a south-westerly direction they would have gone
along the river bank until reaching the slightly protruding lower-
lying areas around the foreshore of the central area. Starting out
at sea, these waves may have been as high as 20 foot by the time
they crashed on to the shore. Buildings near to the Terreiro do
Paço were badly battered – a marble quay in front of the Customs
House was smashed to pieces and the Customs House itself was
badly damaged. In the harbour ships were thrown against each
other; boats on the river were swept away in the current. Hundreds
of people drowned, including groups who had gathered to escape
from the city across the river. By early afternoon, the waves had
subsided, allowing vessels to cross the Tagus once more.

The next disaster to hit the stricken city was fire. Contemporary
accounts seem to suggest that fire broke out in different parts of
the city very soon after the tremors had subsided. Whether these
all arose from natural causes or some were the work of arsonists
who saw an opportunity for looting is not clear. A French deserter
was held responsible for the burning down of the Casa da India.[10]
Little effort was made to try to put the fires out by the exhausted

and demoralized inhabitants who had survived the tremors. Fierce flames soon engulfed the entire central part of the city from the slopes in the ruins of Carmo Convent to the built-up area to the east, under the castle walls. From Rossio Square to the Royal Palace and across to São Paulo, the entire area was gutted. A strong north-west wind spread the flames in an uncontrollable conflagration that lasted for a week before being completely extinguished. Damage from the fire was as great as damage from the earthquake itself.

Lisbon had had a long history of earthquakes; several recorded in the sixteenth century also caused severe damage and loss of life and a tremor in 1750 coincided with the death of King João. The epicentre of the 1755 earthquake was in fact off the coast of Morocco: many cities, including Rabat and Agadir, were damaged by it. Tremors were felt as far away as Brazil and the Antilles, as well as in the south of France and Italy. The two-second tremors registered 9 and 10 on the Mercalli scale, indicating considerable force and likely to cause significant damage. Tremors continued to be felt for some weeks in the Lisbon area, adding to panic and devastation.

The damage done to Lisbon on 1 November 1755 was extensive. Some of the finest civic buildings (including the great trading houses) were ruined; hundreds of smaller shops and homes were destroyed. One estimate suggests that only 3000 of Lisbon's 20,000 houses remained habitable.[11] At least half the city's churches were damaged or reduced to rubble. The riverside, around the Royal Palace in the Terreiro do Paço, was particularly badly affected. The Ribeira Palace itself, crammed with rich artwork and a library that may have numbered 70,000 books, was swept away. The royal family, who were staying in Belém in order to attend Solemn Mass at Jerónimos Church, escaped uninjured. The Bragança Palace, where the crown jewels were kept along with its fine collection of books and works of art, was totally destroyed. Nearby the sumptuous Patriarchal Church and the new Opera House, a

grand, ornate building with gilt interiors that had dazzled the
foreign community and visitors to Lisbon, were both burnt to the
ground. The Opera House had only been opened in the spring. The
Marquis of Louriçal's Renaissance collection of art and another
fine library, which included ancient manuscripts and rare maps
and charts relating to the early voyages of discovery, were also
destroyed. Important collections of incunables in the oratory sited
in the Chiado disappeared in the flames. Gold and other valuables stored in the trading houses were also lost. Foreign traders,
including the English and Hamburg merchants, lost large and
valuable supplies. To east and west the slopes of the city exposed
ruins; perhaps as many as half its buildings were either damaged
or destroyed. Even the Palace of the Inquisition in Rossio Square
had been swept away. Thomas Pitt, an English visitor, soon after
the earthquake records his grim impression:

> A far more melancholy abode than Lisbon cannot be conceived, nothing
> strikes the Eye in the City but ruin and Desolation; the Fire having
> completed what the Earthquake began: Heaps of Rubbish; broken
> walls; Fragments of Churches, with the Paintings and Ornaments in
> many parts remaining, form although a Scene of Horror rather to be
> felt than described.[12]

T.D. Kendrick rightly said that the combined damage of land
movement, flooding and fire amounted to as 'savage a gutting
of the heart of a city as can be found anywhere in the previous
history of Europe'.[13]

It is more difficult to determine how many people were killed
in the disaster. Early reports were wildly exaggerated. In the first
published report that appeared, only six weeks after the event, J.
Trovão e Sousa claimed that as many as 70,000 people had been
killed and much of Lisbon lay in ruins. His totally unscientific
description and gross exaggeration provoked immediate reaction
from other Portuguese writers, who were naturally annoyed at
the impression that this first account was making across Europe.
A number of pamphlets and other works appeared in the early

months of 1756. One of the most reliable is the *Commentary* of António Pereira, who puts the death toll at about 15,000.[14] An attempt was made to count casualties by way of parish records but requests for information sometimes remained unanswered. J.J. Moreira de Mendonça, another of the more reliable historians sets a figure of 5000 deaths on 1 November itself. T.D. Kendrick agrees that António Pereira's figure of 15,000 in total is probably as accurate a guess as is possible.[15] That would have been about 5 per cent of the total population of 275,000.

Many of those killed were caught in churches – either during the first quakes or in subsequent fires while they were sheltering in them.[16] Of the large clerical population only about two hundred probably perished, a relatively small proportion. The British Factory or merchant community, many of whom lived in the suburbs, where the damage was less serious, escaped with a small number of deaths – less than one hundred. D. Francis puts the number at 74.[17] Misery and suffering were, of course widespread. Many people were trapped in rubble, and the dying and injured were left unattended. Crowds of people roamed the streets frightened to go inside the buildings for fear of further tremors, of which many were recorded in subsequent days. Injured animals struggled to free themselves from the wreckage; when freed they faced starvation as there was no one to feed them. The immediate threats to the city were of anarchy and disease.

As the magnitude of the disaster became apparent, an intense debate about its meaning and causes swept across Europe. Voltaire talked of a 'most cruel science' by which 'a hundred thousand of our kindred ants [were] crushed at a blow in our ant heap'.[18] Kendrick says that the earthquake shocked Europeans more than any other event since the collapse of the Roman Empire;[19] a contemporary cleric claimed it was on the scale of the Flood. Such comparisons indicate the degree of shock that the news of the earthquake caused and the profound way in which it was to affect Enlightenment thought.

The conventional clerical view thundered from pulpits within and outside Portugal was that the earthquake was a manifestation of divine wrath. God's anger, it was argued, had been directed against the citizens of one of Europe's major commercial cities because of their addiction to an indulgent and materialistic style of life. The very success of Lisbon, a bustling international centre of trade, had contributed to the disaster. The city was crammed with every imaginable luxury from distant parts: treasuries full of gold, sumptuous collections of exotic objects, slaves from Africa, refined fabrics and rare fruits from distant lands. The outward piety of Lisbon's inhabitants, manifested in their attendance at Mass on the very morning of the disaster, did nothing to balance against the venalities associated with this style of life. Sins had to be punished severely. Some clerics within Portugal tried to mitigate this brutal lesson by suggesting that God had not entirely abandoned his favourites (the Portuguese) and that trust had to be put in his divine mercy, however ineffable it seemed. Others, of a more sadistic inclination, suggested that the Portuguese had in fact been singled out for the honour of punishment in a perverse recognition of their special status in God's eyes. That divine favour had first been made clear by the miraculous appearance of Christ on the battlefield of Ourique in the time of Afonso Henriques. The earthquake, far from being a severe punishment, was an act of love and a more gentle instrument than the wicked citizens of Lisbon really deserved.

The most influential exponents of the theory of unmitigated divine wrath within Portugal were the Jesuits. Their chief spokesman was Gabriel Malagrida,[20] an Italian missionary who had been personally favoured by King João V when he returned to Portugal from Brazil where he had been converting the natives. His reputation for holiness and his connections in aristocratic circles made him a powerful spokesman whose views would carry much weight. In his sermons he concentrated on highlighting the 'abominable sins' of Lisbon folk. When he expanded his argument in a pamphlet, entitled the *Juizo da verdadeira causa do terremoto*, he was particularly contemptuous of any attempt to explain the earthquake in purely natural terms.

> It is scandalous to pretend that the earthquake was just a natural event. For if that be true, there is no need to repent and to try to avert the wrath of God, and not even the Devil himself could invent an idea more likely to lead us to irreparable ruin. Holy people had prophesied that the earthquake was coming, yet the city continued in its sinful ways without a care for the future.[21]

Among the sins indulged in by the citizens of Lisbon which Malagrida listed were theatre-going, (lewd) dancing, watching (obscene) comedies and indulging in the bloody sport of bull fighting. Devoted to these lascivious pastimes, they neglected to fast, scourge and take other devotional steps to prove their obedience to God. They were, in fact, totally irreligious people who would only be saved if they turned to acts of repentance at once. Reconstruction of the city was, by comparison, an unimportant matter. Malagrida thundered:

> Learn, O Lisbon, that the destroyer of our houses, palaces, churches and convents, the cause of the death of so many people and of the flames that devoured such vast treasures, are your abominable sins, and not comets, stars, vapours and exhalations, and similar natural phenomena.[22]

Taking exactly the opposite line, one Portuguese commentator, the Chevalier d'Oliveira, who resided in London and had converted to Protestantism, identified the real problem as the idolatrous practices that Portuguese Catholics *did* observe. Instead of relying on the words of the Bible, his fellow countrymen preferred to rely on the superstitious reverence of saintly images, shrines to the Virgin and other excesses. They tolerated the Office of the Inquisition with its persecution of individuals and minorities such as the Jews. If divine punishment had been meted out, it was because of the existence of this dangerous organization and the superstitions it nurtured among the citizens of Lisbon. The chevalier's pamphlet on the subject, published in 1756, was unsurprisingly proscribed by the Inquisition, but his views were widely shared by many Protestant clerics, including John Wesley, who lashed out against a people he regarded as heathen. According to Wesley, writing a fast-selling pamphlet that was reprinted almost immediately, anyone who thought that the earthquake was not the work of God was denying the authority of Scripture.[23]

The irony of a connection between the piety of the Lisbon churchgoers and the cruel effects of the earthquake, killing innocent and guilty alike, was not lost on Voltaire. In his poem on the disaster he paraded in the most elegant and sombre verse the moral dilemma confronting every European intellectual: how could a benevolent God preside over such a ghastly event? How could anyone henceforth subscribe to the facile belief that all was for the best in this best of all possible worlds when good and bad, guilty and innocent, had all been crushed together? It was utterly useless to tell the victims of the earthquake that somehow it had all been part of God's plan. All that the earthquake showed was the evil inherent in nature (*le Mal est sur la terre*) and the impossibility of explaining it in rational terms at all.

Voltaire went on to explore his theodicy in *Candide* (1759) with such bantering enthusiasm and high spirits that one cannot help suspecting that there is more than a measure of enjoyment in his exposé of moral chaos in the universe. Once again he attacks the absurdity of holding to an optimistic philosophy, which he associates with Leibniz, in the face of disasters of the scale of the earthquake. The pithy tone of the exchange between Pangloss and Candide is a crucial challenge to the optimists.

> Tell me my dear Pangloss, after you had been hanged, dissected, and beaten unmercifully, and while you were rowing at your bench in the galley, were you still convinced that everything in this world was for the best?

Pangloss replies:

I stick to my original views because I am a philosopher. It would be wrong for me to recant especially since Leibniz could not have been wrong. Pre-established harmony, together with the *plenum* and the *materia subtilis*, is the most beautiful thing on earth.[24]

Reading *Candide*, one is left with the distinct impression that Voltaire is questioning not only the existence of a benevolent God but the existence of a God at all. The conclusion that faith alone can sustain man in the face of such irrationality as the earthquake rings a very hollow note indeed. The secular lesson that he wished to impart was that instead of trying to unravel such imponderables – those causes of things that Dr Pangloss spends so much time puzzling over – man was better off applying his reason to solving the social and economic problems that beset the majority of his fellows. Only in that way could he tackle the problem of alleviating evil.

Despite this intellectual onslaught the optimists did reply. Most prominently Jean-Jacques Rousseau challenged Voltaire's conclusions head-on.[25] He says that physical evil must be distinguished from moral evil. Physical evil is part of the natural order – it is inherent in the great chain of being where some creatures are superior to others and may live off those below themselves. In the case of moral evil, man himself is the principal culprit. But even in respect of physical evil, man is to blame for much of what happens. Agreeing with Voltaire that it would have been better if the earthquake had occurred in a desert, Rousseau points out that in fact earthquakes do occur in such places but pass unnoticed. Man's folly was in building populous cities like Lisbon, with its 20,000 or so six-storey buildings, concentrated in a small area where the effects of an earthquake were bound to be catastrophic. If the city had been more dispersed, if its citizens had not remained in it because of their fear of losing property and possessions after the first tremor had occurred, the loss of life would have been far less. Man cannot defy the laws of nature without paying a heavy price. But he should not give up belief in a benevolent God who mitigated the effects of evil and provided a basis for hope in a better future. Rousseau ends by comparing his optimism in difficult circumstance of life to Voltaire's pessimism in easy ones, even though he pays tribute to the great philosopher.

Another philosopher who came to the conclusion that man had to live according to the laws of nature was Immanuel Kant. But in the hands of the young Kant, the explanation took on a more scientific flavour. Earthquakes were natural phenomena to be explained by scientific laws. A philosopher had to understand the causes and operation of those laws. It was absurd to try to deduce divine motivation from such a happening as an earthquake. It was a natural occurrence, which could produce good, as well as bad, effects. In any case the suffering of the Lisbon citizens could be exaggerated. Everyone had to die sooner or later; all property was eventually lost to its owners or destroyed. This theme was repeated by less well-known writers who questioned whether many deaths at once were any worse than single deaths one by one. In times of disaster, men forgot the long periods of calm that they enjoyed in normal times. No doubt the great city of Lisbon would be rebuilt and in a better form than it had been before. Nevertheless the earthquake itself raised fundamental doubts about the relation of God and man.

Fernando Pessoa captures the extreme scepticism that this conclusion may lead to in the words of Ricardo Reis very much later. His tone is of a modernist Voltaire.

> My act when I destroy
> The structure ants have raised
> Must seem to them divine indeed
> Yet in my own eyes I am not divine.
> Perhaps, just so, the gods
> No gods in their own eyes
> Merely because they are greater than we
> Appear as gods in ours.
> Be the truth as it may
> Even towards those

Whom we consider gods, let us not be
Perfect in a faith that may be groundless.[26]

While the lofty debates of the *philosophes* raged across Europe, within Portugal a small group of men were determined to spread word through the international community that Lisbon had survived a catastrophe and was open for trade. They realized that to do that convincingly they had to take action to ensure that normal life in the city could be resumed as speedily as possible. António Pereira mentions the actions of four prominent citizens who contributed to the restoration of order and confidence – namely the Duke of Lafões, who as head of civil administration worked tirelessly to preserve law and order; his younger brother, Dom João de Bragança, who took a lead in rescue work; the old Cardinal Patriarch Manuel; and Monsenhor Sampaio of the Patriarchal Church, who, with numerous other clergymen, had stayed at their posts and continued to administer to the spiritual needs of the citizens. Mendonça mentions[27] the generosity of the royal princes Palhavã (the bastard sons of King João V) and, most important of all, the secretary of state, Carvalho e Melo, later to become the Marquis of Pombal.[28]

Pombal was the real genius behind the impressive effort to get Lisbon functioning again. Brushing aside all suggestions of abandoning the capital, he realized that the administration had to seize the initiative if civil disorder on a serious scale was to be averted.[29] His ruthless realism is summarized in the advice given to the king to 'bury the dead and feed the living'. Pombal realized that to achieve success government had to be directed to clear and precise policy objectives. Planning needed to be detailed and effective; policy would only gain widespread support if it appeared to apply to all citizens alike of whatever station. Ironically the minister's own house, in the Rua Formosa, had survived the quakes. When the king remarked that this was a divine dispensation, the Count of São Lourenço, Pombal's enemy, declared that the principal street in the red-light district had also survived.[30]

Pombal divided Lisbon into twelve administrative districts, each headed by a magistrate who was responsible for ensuring that newly drawn up emergency measures were enacted. The first and most urgent need was to dispose of the dead. The most efficient method of disposing of corpses was to take them on barges, which were then sunk in the Tagus. Strongly anti-clerical by instinct, the secretary of state nevertheless realized that he needed the support of the Church and got the Cardinal Patriarch's agreement to this unconventional method of burial. If the bodies had not been dealt with quickly, plague or other disease would have soon broken out. Several medical men spoke out about the need for the quick disposal of corpses, although others claimed that the risks were being exaggerated by the authorities. They pointed out the beneficial effects of the fires in that respect, since they amounted to wholesale, sanitary cremation of the population buried in the ruins. Pombal's efforts on public health were helped by the cool winter weather which followed the earthquake.

Pombal made the central control of the administration so tight that the next vital matter, securing a safe water supply, could be put into immediate effect. Of equal importance was ensuring sufficient food supplies. Warehouses and other places where food had been left were requisitioned; cooks, millers and other involved in catering were compelled to work in specially set up centres. Food prices were controlled, particularly by the lifting of tax on fish, the staple diet. The supply of fuel, particularly wood, was also controlled centrally. Response from abroad also helped these considerable efforts. The British Parliament voted £50,000 of aid; supplies of fuel and provisions were sent from Spain and much needed timber from the Hanseatic League based in Hamburg.[31]

The practical measures were supplemented by a strict enforcement of law and order. Chief magistrates had the power to order summary execution of anyone who was caught looting or pillaging. At least 34 people were executed for such offences within the first few days of November. The movement of individuals was also controlled so that people in particularly vital jobs – carpenters and builders for example – could be kept in the city or returned from the provinces if they were found to have fled from the metropolis. Bands of workmen were forced to the urgent job of removing rubble and flattening buildings that were too dangerous to leave standing. At the same time a survey of property was instituted, as disputes about ownership were likely to arise once the initial shock of what had happened had been absorbed. In some areas, of course, nothing remained to be recorded. These measures were seen to be just and gained the minister widespread support for his strict control of the lives of citizens who had been accustomed to a degree of freedom in going about their business.

To help the economy stabilize, rents and wages were controlled and a massive programme of house building was undertaken. This reconstruction moved on at a very rapid pace. The king and his court had taken to living in tents soon after 1 November but within months a wooden building had been put up on the site of the Ajuda Palace. It remained the royal residence until 1777. So far as more modest housing was concerned, as many as 9000 wooden structures were put up in six months, housing a proportion of the 25,000 refugee population. The building programme was carefully planned from the centre; no construction work was allowed to proceed without permission. Pombal realized that the flattening of a large part of the riverside area and levelling some of the hillside to the west would enable a new modern city to be built around the Baixa district. He was determined that this would be done in an orderly manner. The layout would be on a grid system, making downtown Lisbon one of the most up-to-date Enlightenment cities, a home fit for a new middle class on whom national prosperity would depend.

A team of engineers and architects, including Manuel da Maia, Carlos Mardel and Eugénio dos Santos (all military officers), took as their starting point the great square or Terreiro do Paço where the Ribeira Palace had stood.[32] The idea of focusing the city's centre on a great square at the waterfront was dos Santos's idea; significantly it was to be renamed Commercial Square.[33] A grand equestrian statue in bronze of the king in triumphal mode, clutching his sceptre, the symbol of absolute power, was later erected in the square. From the square two parallel roads, the Rua Aurea and the Rua Augusta sweep straight up to Rossio, whilst just to the east the grid leads through another set of streets, parallel with the Rua da Prata, to the Praça da Figueira. The whole area forms an impressive rectangle and has remained the commercial and financial centre of the city to the present day. Street lighting and other modern conveniences were installed under the imaginative superintendence of Pina Manique, one of Pombal's close allies.[34]

Pombal's policies were executed not only for the benefit of the citizens of Lisbon but to restore the confidence of the international trading community upon whom Portugal depended for its economic welfare. The message for them was that not only would their interests be protected but in fact the reconstruction of Lisbon would enhance the possibilities of commerce.[35] Pombal had been much influenced by his diplomatic career, which had been spent in London and, from there, in Vienna. In 1739 he had replaced his cousin, Mario António de Azevedo, as the envoy to the Court of St James's. Pombal was never entirely at home in England – his grasp of the language was not fluent even though he moved in erudite circles such as the Royal Society. Nevertheless, he recognized the superiority of English commercial arrangements, particularly the organization of the great trading companies, whose ships had the protection of the Royal Navy when carrying out their overseas enterprises.

Pombal particularly resented the British monopoly of the Brazilian trade. These interests were protected by two treaties, one agreed in 1654 during Cromwell's dictatorship, the other signed in 1703 and known as the Methuen Treaty. These treaties not only guaranteed special access for British ships to Brazilian ports, but exempted British goods from certain customs duties.

British merchants understood that the Brazilian trade was one that needed medium- to long-term investment. What is more, they had sufficient capital resources to fund credit over a number years, giving them an edge over Portuguese rivals. Average profits of sale from this colonial trade could be as high as 30 per cent, double the already profitable 15 per cent made in Portugal itself.[36]

It seemed to Pombal that the British had done too well out of these arrangements and he was determined to claw back advantages for Portugal. As the representative of his country at the Court of St James's, he pressed hard for recognition of Portuguese commercial interests and gained some minor success for Portuguese residents in Britain.[37] His London days taught him how demanding the English could be when it came to trading terms and how much the old alliance served British, rather than Portuguese, interests. When he returned to Portugal, Pombal began to consider ways of curbing British privileges without upsetting an alliance upon which Portuguese foreign policy had been firmly based for decades. British support was meant to be a guarantee against incursion by Spain, seen as a threat and one that was realized in 1762. The Royal Navy also guaranteed the integrity of Brazil. Pombal would have had some sympathy with the view expressed by the French writer Ange Goudar that the Portuguese should take the opportunity afforded by the rebuilding of Lisbon to throw off what was an oppressive British control of their affairs. But the minister knew that Portugal still depended on British protection in the event of a threat from Spain.[38]

In his reconstruction of Lisbon after the earthquake, Pombal applied the lessons he had learnt in London, giving due prominence to the interests of the commercial houses. The new grid system designed for the Baixa allowed for the orderly coordination of commercial, banking and government interests. Buildings were to be in uniform style, with limited ornamentation on their façades. Arcaded elevations and pavilions echoed the neo-Palladian style popular in England. By keeping the design simple (the so-called

'Pombalese' fronts were plainer than previous styles) much of the
work could be prefabricated and put into place speedily and more
economically than would otherwise have been the case.

William Dalrymple, staying in Lisbon in 1774, records a favourable impression of the Baixa:

> In whole streets and adjoining squares were planned in a single sweep:
> there was no place for individual variation. This effect was immedi-
> ately apparent to visitors, in the New City there is great attention to
> uniformity, and the houses being built of white stone have a beautiful
> appearance.[39]

Plainer façades would have lent an air of harmony to the emerging clean-cut buildings. The uniform feeling was also achieved by
strict measurement of the streets – 60 foot across for those running
up the grid north to south; 40 foot across for those crossing west to
east. Pavements of exact proportions were laid out on each street.
The military background of the team of engineers and surveyors
in charge of reconstruction was clearly in evidence in this preci-
sion planning. The very proximity and modernity of the quarter
encouraged efficiency; new safety for buildings was provided by
the invention of a flexible wooden frame, known as the *gaiola*,
around which the structure was built. This reinforcement was
intended to make them more resistant to future tremors.[40] Other
features included a new sewerage system and wherever possible
fountains for the provision of clean water. These amenities were
attractive to those commercial businesses that were largely to
finance the rebuilding.

However, Pombal's reforms went further than mere physical rebuilding. He set about changing the conditions of employment and
practices in the public service. Realizing that the public service
needed to be more effective in a modern, commercial country, he
turned his attention to the education system from which he would
recruit a new class of bureaucrats inspired by modernizing ideals.
If this meant more openness and recruitment by merit, he was
prepared for it. Towards this end, he established new institutions

such as the Casa do Risco das Reais Obras – a school of architecture and drawing – and the Colégio Real dos Nobres where classes were held on the principles of military and civil architecture. In 1770 the Junta de Providência Literária began to formulate new statutes for the University of Coimbra. The emphasis of these reforms was to promote the study of science, and various buildings in the university were to be dedicated to that purpose.[41] In this enterprise, as in others, Pombal did not hesitate to act radically to achieve his ends.

Meanwhile the ex-envoy turned his mind to ways of mitigating the trading advantages which he had seen so effortlessly enjoyed by the British. A careful reading of old treaties, particularly that of 1654, proved fruitful. Pombal soon realized that under the terms of the agreement, the British Factory only controlled the wine trade in the absence of the existence of any Portuguese company. However, if one were to be set up, it would have the right to deal exclusively with the wine trade to Brazil. Accordingly, in 1756, Pombal set up the Douro Wine Company with a monopoly over the wine business and thereby gained control of a trade which had always been entirely in British hands.

Although scoring advantages over the British would not have upset them, Pombal's radicalism at home unsettled members of the old court nobility, who saw him as a menace to their conservative way of life. Not only did they regard him socially inferior but they considered that meritocratic educational views would eventually loosen the grip which their own families held on privileged positions at home and in the colonies. For his part Pombal was concerned as for the progress of the nation and had no patience for those who did not share his ideal. However, his position was still precarious as he depended entirely on royal favour. Although his success in tackling the considerable problems that had resulted from the earthquake had put him in a powerful position, he still needed to consolidate it by removing opposition from the old aristocrats.

The minister's chance came in 1758 when a group of conservative nobles attempted a *coup d'état*. An attempt was made to assassinate King José I, whom the rebels considered to be entirely under the minister's control. The king was only wounded in the attempt on his life but seriously enough for the queen to assume a regency during his convalescence. Dom José, enfeebled by years of sybaritic living (his two passions were hunting and the Italian opera, on which he had lavished royal funds), had no idea how to handle a situation he had not anticipated. He could only turn to his first minister, who had shown such steeliness in dealing with the earthquake. Pombal acted ruthlessly. After an initial period of silence, a series of arrests were made. Members of the Tavora family (headed by the Duke of Aveiro) and the Count of Atouguia were the most prominent of those detained, but Pombal also took the chance to act against the Jesuits by confining leading members of the order to house arrest. A tribunal was set up with sweeping powers; Pombal as the minister responsible for home affairs sat on it personally and took part in the interrogation of the prisoners. Proceedings were conducted in secret. A panel of judges, over whom Pombal also had control, pronounced sentence for the crime of treason. All the leading conspirators, including the Duke of Aveiro, were summarily executed. Their families were rounded up, tortured and in some cases left in prison for years.

Acting against the Jesuits would take a little longer. Pombal had first clashed with the Jesuits in Brazil, setting up his company the Junta do Comércio to break the missionaries' stranglehold on the country. As he encountered the force of their resistance, the minister came to realize that only by removing the order altogether would he secure crown interests entirely. He therefore undertook a policy of expelling the order from various provinces in Brazil until they were no longer able to operate in the country at all. Emboldened by his success, Pombal turned his attention to the metropolis. By 1759 he had persuaded the king that the Jesuits were a menace to national security, and they were duly expelled.

Pombal began a policy which was followed in a number of European countries: in France in 1764 and in Spain in 1767. In 1773 Pope Clement XIV decreed a suppression of the entire order.

However, Pombal was not yet finished with the Jesuits. He despised Padre Gabriel Malagrida, their leader, for supporting, as we have seen, the widespread theological view that the earthquake was a sign of God's wrath and a punishment for the hedonistic life of the inhabitants of Lisbon. With his considerable personal authority, Malagrida had flatly contradicted Pombal's view that the earthquake was a natural phenomenon. This was open defiance and something Pombal could not let pass if his authority was to remain intact. Malagrida's view undermined his entire reform programme, which was based on a rational response to a natural rather than divinely inspired happening. Once his overtures to Rome failed, Pombal turned to the Portuguese clergy. Having installed his brother to head the Inquisition, he persuaded senior Portuguese clerics to take up the case against Malagrida. He was now pursued as both a heretic and a subject in rebellion against the crown, although the evidence against him was thin. The Inquisition was persuaded of his guilt and ordered punishment. Malagrida was eventually garrotted and publicly burnt in Lisbon in 1761.

Pombal's action in the matter of the Aveiro conspiracy displayed the same ruthless realpolitik that he had employed after the earthquake. The decade that followed the Lisbon earthquake marked the high point of his influence. He himself ascended to the rank of marquis and ruled the country as a dictator, though he depended entirely on royal backing. His energies were directed at modernizing Portugal along English and Dutch lines. The king allowed him a free hand, even acceding to the minister's requests that royal expenditure should be more tightly controlled. Although Pombal may have acted ruthlessly against those who opposed him and favoured those who supported him, his measures on the whole stabilized the Portuguese economy after the excesses of the first half of the century under King João V. In the two decades of his rule he had done much to put Portugal on the path to being a modern state, capable of competing against its European rivals. The earthquake had proved the decisive turning point in providing the opportunity for this short-lived period of enlightened despotism.

5

Foreigners' City

Lisbon has been a foreigners' city from ancient times. Waves of new races and tribes have come across the Iberian mainland or by sea to settle, for the most part harmoniously, by the shores of the Tagus. The indigenous Iberian stock, probably settled long before, is already in evidence during the Paleolithic Age. The first overseas arrivals were the Phoenicians, followed by the Greeks and then by the Celts, who had made their way overland. All of these people were attracted to the advantages of living along a large river estuary, with plentiful supplies of fish in the ocean and a fertile hinterland for the production of food. By the time of the Roman occupation in the first century BC, these various races had already been mingled together to form a complex mix.

The arrival of the Romans added another layer to this cosmopolitan base. Thracians, Cretans, Jews and North Africans came to Portugal and Spain in the service of their Latin masters. Slaves, upon whom the economy of the empire depended, were brought in from across the Mediterranean, adding to what was already a racial melting pot. When the Roman Empire collapsed, as we have seen,

Germanic tribes invaded Iberia.[1] The Suevi came to Portugal and intermingled with the diverse local population; they were followed by the Moors, who ruled Balata, as the province became known, for 500 years. By the time of the Moorish invasion of the eighth century, the Jewish community was already well established, playing a major role in the commercial life of the city. Mozarabic society showed all the signs of fusion found in sophisticated, cosmopolitan communities. When Moorish rule formally ended, a large population of Mudejar citizens (those of Muslim faith) remained. They were to contribute significantly to many arts and sciences, such as ceramics and irrigation, in the country of their birth.

The liberation of Lisbon by Afonso Henriques in 1147 was accomplished with the help of many foreign mercenaries, among whom the English were prominent, but French and German and Flemish crusaders also featured. These foreign supporters needed to be rewarded, whether, as in the case of Gilbert of Hastings, with clerical posts or, as in other cases, with grants of land from the crown. Records of land ownership show foreign names among the Portuguese during the early years of the nation. As Lisbon itself expanded as an international centre of commerce, other foreign communities arrived. Among these were Italians – both Venetian and Genoese merchants began to play a significant part in trading activities, whilst other Italians arrived to meet the demand for artists, sculptors and craftsmen with specialized skills. As the crown and aristocracy became wealthier, they commissioned ambitious building projects. Foreign architects arrived to build as well as to embellish the churches and palaces of Lisbon.

The crusaders who came to the service of Afonso Henriques were little more than hardened adventurers, seeking new opportunities in life. The English in particular were known for their harsh manners and debauched behaviour. They may have been rivalled in these proclivities by the Franks and Germans. The northern invaders came from the same lands as those barbarians who had brought down the Roman Empire. According to the flowery account given by Osbern of Bawdsey, a fighting priest, these rough men were persuaded to stay and fight for the Portuguese cause because of the persuasive words of the Bishop of Oporto and the Archbishop of Braga.[2] The bishops strengthened their case by an appeal to the material, as well as spiritual, advantages that would come the way of those supporting their cause. Good wine and other venal delights would be immediate but the promise of the possession of some of the gentle, fertile land, which made up the hinterland of the city, sharpened appetites for the fight. A further stimulus was the rumour that hoards of gold and silver were hidden in the city waiting for its liberators to seize as booty.

Nevertheless the crusaders faced a considerable challenge. Not only was Lisbon well fortified, but its position on hilly slopes, near the river's edge, made it difficult to attack from any direction. The streets of the city were steep; the citadel which crowned the highest ridge, housing the Moorish palace and headquarters, was particularly inaccessible. Several of the foreign leaders began to talk of months of siege, which would result in their losing the easier pickings that might be made along the Mediterranean coasts or even in the Holy Land itself. Despite these reservations they stayed and a long siege began. As the summer advanced, the inhabitants of the city were reduced to starvation. Added to the extreme discomfort of the sweltering weather was disease brought on by unhygienic conditions. Plague decimated the ranks of attackers and defenders alike. Whenever anyone was captured, on either side, rough justice was meted out. When the crusaders finally breached the defences and got into the city, rape and pillage became the order of the day. It had taken seventeen long, gruelling weeks to reach that point.

Gilbert of Hastings, installed as Bishop of Lisbon, was the first of a long line of Englishmen who were to play a prominent role in the public life of the new nation. Gilbert seemed the perfect candidate for the post – pious and learned, he also proved to be a good administrator. His reputation ensured that a number of English chaplains decided to remain in Lisbon to serve under him. He even

managed to integrate the Templars, notoriously independent, into
his fold. The king rewarded the churchmen – 32 houses, farmland,
fruit groves and vineyards were handed over to the bishop. This
made for a good start but Gilbert was not idle. He reorganized
the area into a large diocese that spread eastwards to Evora and
southwards to Alcácer do Sal. He took a lead in encouraging the
programme to build Lisbon Cathedral. Instead of persecuting
Moorish inhabitants of the city, he attempted to convert them
to Christianity. Sometimes his interventions failed – he could
not persuade the crusaders to stay on in order to capture Alcácer
do Sal, with its strongly fortified citadel (it was eventually taken
in 1218). In the case of other towns that were captured, such as
Silves in 1189, he was unable to prevent indiscriminate massacre
and pillage from taking place.

The English influence, begun with the crusaders' intervention
in the liberation of Lisbon, continued throughout the early period
of Portugal's history as a nation. It was consolidated by a dynastic
alliance between King João I and Philippa of Lancaster, which
followed the signing of the Treaty of Windsor in 1386. King João
himself had inaugurated a new style of monarchy, more absolutist
in nature, in which the aristocracy, endowed with estates, was
closely dependent on the crown. The alliance with England, which
was to be 'perpetual', was an important symbol of royal influence
abroad. Part of the agreement was that the Portuguese king should
support the English claim to the Castilian throne, but as this
faded away as a political objective, the benefit of a link which
would protect Portugal from Castilian invasion seemed even more
important.[3] The English alliance would, at the very least, make
the Spanish think twice before attempting a takeover. Philippa
arrived with a large entourage of courtiers and craftsmen, including disciples of the master builder William of Wykeham, whose
influence became visible in local ecclesiastical architecture. Her
chancellor was Adam Davenport; important posts at court were
filled by his fellow countrymen.

Cultivated and gracious, the queen set the tone for a well-ordered, courteous court, which sometimes sat at Sintra, her favourite place. Writers, artists and poets were encouraged to mix with the courtiers; soon there was intermarriage between Philippa's English followers and the Portuguese *fidalgo* families. The English connection also proved a stimulant to trade. English merchants began to see the ease of carrying on business in a country where they were so advantageously placed. Lisbon also benefited from this new cosmopolitan influx, expanding along the river westwards in new, elegant suburbs. The queen's intellectual interests were passed on to the royal princes. Duarte turned writer, producing his treatise on public law, the *Leal Conselheiro*, whilst Prince Henry began a lifelong interest in mathematics and navigational studies, with highly significant consequences for Portugal's development as a maritime nation, as we have seen.[4]

Other foreigners continued to live in Lisbon alongside the Jews and Moors for many generations after the founding of the nation. A significant influx came with the Manueline expansion of the city in the early sixteenth century. Trade with the east had brought Lisbon enormous wealth; commercial communities from all over Europe wanted to share in this prosperity. Moreover they brought with them specialized knowledge – in commerce and in banking – which would be of enormous benefit to Portugal. Among the most prominent groups were the Italian merchants who specialized in every aspect of maritime business. Lucas Giraldes was a sixteenth-century Florentine banker whose Lisbon interests were so successful that he was able to set himself up in some style in Sintra whither the aristocrats followed the court during the summer months.

Meanwhile the English Factory continued to strengthen its grip on trading between the two nations. Merchants were protected by the terms of treaties that pre-dated the Treaty of Windsor and subsequent agreements made between Edward I and King Dinis in the thirteenth century. Wine, olive oil, cork, salt and fruits were exported from Portugal, while wool, cloth, lead and tin were imported from England. As trade became brisker, the English presence grew and English merchants benefited from the experience of a long-established community. Although traders from both countries came to understand each other, and crucially how to operate within two different spheres of law, there was friction. English merchants complained about the slow clearance of goods through customs, corruption in handling charges and the return of confiscated property in a worse condition than it had been when it had been seized. When legal disputes did arise, the Portuguese courts were accused of acting in a biased and unfair manner. Nevertheless trade between the two countries was too important to be damaged by minor wrangles. The Casa da India, the largest of the Lisbon depots (where spices, sugar, molasses and silks were crammed into the vaults), was the largest warehouse in the world; access to it was the guarantee of wealth and fortune.

Whilst the English merchant community was getting well established, other non-commercial institutions were also becoming embedded in the fabric of Lisbon life. One of these was the Bridgetine nunnery, which was founded in 1594. The nuns originated from Isleworth, near London, but had left the country after the dissolution of the monasteries in 1536. For the next half-century they moved around different countries in Europe until they reached Lisbon. At first regarded with some suspicion by the Portuguese episcopal hierarchy, the nuns were nevertheless received civilly and provided with a house in the city. From then on, the sisters remained in Lisbon for almost three hundred years, benefiting from Spanish patronage and the sale of their home-made confectionery. They were highly thought of by locals and visitors alike. In the late eighteenth century Joseph Barretti described them as charming company. There was no impetus for them to return to England until the start of the Napoleonic Wars, when things started to become difficult and dangerous for any British inhabitant of the

:ity. A nucleus remained, amalgamating with their Irish holy sisters for greater security, and survived until the middle of the nineteenth century.

Another English Catholic institution in the city was the English College, founded in 1622. After a struggle with the Jesuits who had set up the Residency, the College retained its independence, although it came under the general supervision of the Inquisitor General. Its teachers came from Douai; its students were known as the 'Inglesinhos' (young Englishmen) and cut a distinct figure in their black cassocks on the streets of the city. Their ostensible devotion to combating heresy among their fellow countrymen earned them the protection of the Portuguese establishment.

Outside the institution, individual priests also made their mark. Father Daniel O'Daly was installed as rector of the Dominican Convent in 1634. O'Daly was an Irish patriot with no love of England; he received financial support from the Spanish royal family, as well as acting as confessor to the Spanish queen of Portugal. These connections made him the object of suspicion among the English community. So impressive was his ability to get resources that he was able to found the Convent of Bom Sucesso, which played an important role in the clerical life of the city thereafter.

Bishop Richard Russell was a very different, but equally successful, cleric. He started life at the English College as a servant but soon proved his intellectual credentials by qualifying for a studentship, which took him to Douai. He was ordained a priest in Paris, returning to Lisbon to be installed as procurator at his old college. Russell's linguistic ability was considerable; he was chosen to accompany Francisco de Melo, the Portuguese envoy in London, on a mission to extend British military aid to Portugal. Russell must have been a man of some charm; he soon became a royal favourite and the outcome of the diplomatic mission was to begin the elaborate negotiations that ended with Catherine of Bragança becoming the wife of King Charles II. Russell was made Bishop of Portalegre in 1671 as a reward for his part in bringing about the dynastic alliance. His parishioners were not disappointed by his command of Portuguese.

If English Catholics played some role in the development of Anglo-Portuguese relations, the majority of their fellow countrymen, as Protestants, came under the ministry of the chaplain to the English Factory. The right for Englishmen to practise their own religion had been enshrined in the Cromwellian Treaty of 1654. Nevertheless relations with the Catholic Church proved difficult. The administrators of the Inquisition were particularly hostile to allowing the holding of Protestant services at all; in the event the best they could do was to confine them to the British envoy's house.

Sometimes relations between the chaplain and his parishioners could be stormy. The Reverend John Colbatch, who held the post in the seventeenth century, railed against the lax moral standards of members of the Factory or commercial community. His particular target was the envoy himself, John Methuen, who declared himself to be a disciple of the ungodly Thomas Hobbes. Not only did Methuen spend his time reading *Leviathan* but he also disregarded holy days, dining in style on Good Friday and, even worse, carrying on a fairly open affair with the consul's wife. As if to goad the chaplain further, he also agreed with the view of the Inquisition that Protestant services could only be conducted in his residence, so that when he was out of town services were suspended.

Whatever Methuen's devotion to Hobbes, he was at the same time laying the foundations for a new British hegemony by securing the incipient port wine business for the English merchants of Oporto. As the demand for port grew at the expense of the standard table wine, Red Portugal (which had come from the Minho), the English trading houses were firmly established as the sole regulators of the trade. Importation of Portuguese wine was to be balanced against the export of English cloth. Methuen returned to London, leaving negotiations in the hands of his son. They were successfully concluded in a second treaty of a mere two

articles, which bear the family name, in 1703. Meanwhile Colbatch, who seems to have got on better with the young Methuen,
approached Bishop Burnet of Salisbury, his patron, to seek official
condemnation of the elder Methuen. The Bishop must have been
a wily politician who understood that challenging the very man
who had just secured the country an advantageous treaty would
be a waste of time. He refused to intervene. Colbatch returned
to England, where he published his memoirs about his time in
Portugal.[5]

British influence in Portugal was consolidated by the growth of
the port wine trade, now protected by the terms of the Methuen
Treaty. The trade was based in Oporto where the English built an
impressive Factory House, held grand banquets and played cricket
in the nearby fields. The port wine trade, as Pombal realized,
became a vital part of the Portuguese economy, so that benefits
were felt throughout the country, including the city of Lisbon
through which much of the trade flowed. This economic interest
was matched by the political alliance between Britain and Portugal. For the Portuguese the alliance was meant to guarantee the
country's territorial integrity; for the British it provided a toehold
on the continent of Europe. Ironically it was eventually the threat
from France, rather than Spain, which consolidated the British grip
on Portugal at the time of the Napoleonic Wars. But successive
British envoys had the ear of the Portuguese monarch of the day,
on account of the strong trade links between the two countries and
the dependency of Portugal on Britain for its territorial security.

Throughout the eighteenth century a succession of British
tourists, clergymen, soldiers and businessmen passed through
the country on visits of various lengths. They recounted their
experiences in books, pamphlets and letters home. Sometimes,
like Richard Twiss, they described the social structure of the
country; at other times, as in the case of James Murphy, they
dwelt on buildings and styles of architecture.[6] Towards the end
of the century a trio of outstanding literary figures – William

Beckford, Robert Southey and Lord Byron – came to set the seal
of romanticism on a little-known corner of Europe.

William Beckford arrived in Lisbon in March 1787 on his way
to visit family estates in Jamaica, a journey that he never completed. He arrived in Portugal in some style – with a retinue of
servants, furniture and books, which caused a great stir in the
city. The French ambassador noted the princely income of this
English 'milord' with some envy.[7] Within a short time of his arrival, Beckford was introduced to the influential Marialva family,
the head of which was traditionally appointed Master of the Horse
with direct access to the monarch.[8] Surprisingly, Beckford's first
description of Pombalese Lisbon is not favourable; like Fielding
he complained about the jumbled, medieval aspect of its skyline.
The large, conventual buildings towered above what seemed to be a
string of villages perched on various hills. Nor did he seem pleased
with the interior of Portuguese houses, finding the Marialva Palace
along the west coast sparsely furnished, without much taste. James
Murphy was to remark that many aristocratic Portuguese families
were, in fact, quite hard up despite owning landed estates outside
the city and being accompanied everywhere by bevies of servants
and hangers-on.[9] This would have explained something of the
austerity of the interiors that Beckford saw.

Nevertheless Beckford was impressed by the semi-feudal manner
of the Marialvas' home life. There were interminable meals, always
attended upon by scores of servants and hangers-on, with musical
entertainment provided. Beckford had a covert interest in the
family, which arose because of its connection with the queen.
He himself had had to leave England under the cloud of a homo-
sexual scandal; by being presented at a foreign court he might
begin to make the comeback into the upper echelons of English
society which he was so keen to do. His efforts were thwarted by
Robert Walpole, the British envoy, who may have been acting from
instructions from home or may merely have been venting his spleen
against a young, attractive millionaire. The intrigue surrounding

this affair, with the Marquis of Marialva championing Beckford's cause, is recorded in a private journal Beckford kept during the blazing Lisbon summer of 1787.[10]

One aspect of Lisbon life that enthralled Beckford was the spectacular religious ceremonies that were performed regularly. Soon after his arrival he attended the consecration of the Bishop of the Algarve at the Convent of the Necessidades amid a 'mighty glitter of capes, censures, mitres and croziers continually in motion'.[11] Only a few days later came the festival of Corpo de Deus, when the Patriarch of Lisbon led a glittering procession of clerics through the streets of the city. The patriarch himself was borne forward like a pontiff under a great arched canopy, while the priests and acolytes who followed were dressed in magnificent ceremonial robes. Cannons blasted from the castle; church bells peeled across the city decked in flowers; crowds swarmed about to watch the progress of this majestic procession. The pomp and circumstance of the occasion appealed much to Beckford's sense of theatre. The elaborate Masses, sometimes held in the sumptuous church attached to the Patriarchal Seminary, also appealed to his sensuous nature. Devoting himself to St Anthony, the English visitor began to attract attention to himself for his own public displays of piety.

Beckford moved in the highest aristocratic circles. His descriptions of life in the *ancien régime* are regarded by Portuguese historians as important sources about the life of the court aristocracy. Among the palaces he visited in Lisbon was that of the Palhavã princes, bastard offspring of King João V. The princes, who by the time of Beckford's stay in Portugal were in their sixties, had led a sheltered and dreary existence, dragged out in the fusty and gloomy apartments of their palace. Beckford spares no effect in re-creating its atmosphere of heaviness, noting the dark crimson draperies and the heavy scent of burnt lavender which hung in the stale air and was sickening. No one could imagine that there was much pleasure in the lives of these now elderly princes, who, as royalty, had to observe the stiff etiquette of the court.

Other company was more cheerful and interesting: Beckford
derived a great deal of amusement from the company of the Duke
of Lafões, who though older than the Palhavã princes was sprightly
and high-spirited.[12] The duke was the epitome of a dandy, speaking
in a lisping French and parading the privileges of his old, noble
line. A more sombre personage was the second Marquis of Pombal,
the great man's son, who came to visit Beckford. Although 'worn
down with gambling and lechery' he was possessed of 'an ease and
fashion in his address not common in Portugal'.[13] Although Pombal
seemed to have any amount of credit, he confided in Beckford
that his father had died in debt. Both sons of famous politicians,
who were never accepted in the highest circles, the two men had
much in common.

Although Beckford spent some time in Sintra, he returned in
1793 to live in his old house in the Rua Cova da Moura rented to
him on his first visit. Its location suited him perfectly. Situated
to the west of Lisbon, somewhat away from Buenos Ayres, the
favoured residence of the British, it was near to the royal palace
of Necessidades, something that appealed to Beckford's snobbish
sense. It was also within easy reach of the coast and of the valley of
Alcântara, where he liked to ride. Like many other post-earthquake
buildings the house was made of wood. Beckford regarded it as a
'paste board' habitation, which he wanted to replace with a more
substantial property reflecting his position in Lisbon society. He
therefore moved to a villa at Belém, a little further west, and
started planning for a grand mansion, with salons and wings, on
the site of the wooden house. His drawings for this house illustrate
how his ideas were developing and hint at the plan he would later
follow at Fonthill Abbey, his grandest project.[14]

Beckford's accounts of Lisbon society and his creation of a
Romantic Sintra setting had a lasting effect on the imagination of
the Portuguese. His role as a dashing and lordly English figure of
immense wealth added to his legendary status. Most nineteenth-
century Portuguese came to know about him through periodicals

hat enjoyed a wide middle-class readership. Like the readers of travel accounts in England, these bourgeois Portuguese hankered after tales from the more spacious days of the *ancien régime*. Beckford's portrayal of aristocratic life was sufficiently decadent, while his connection with the royal family appealed to their snobbish sense. In 1863 Rebelo da Silva, who was both novelist and historian, introduced a Beckfordian hero into his story *Lágrimas e Tesouros*, portraying him as a man of mystery and imagination. In this way Beckford joined the canon of foreign Romantics, historical and fantastic, like Byron and Werther.[15]

In contrast to most English visitors who arrived on the 'Packet' at Lisbon harbour, Robert Southey came overland from Spain, crossing into the country at Elvas. Compared to the arid plain of Castile, Portugal at once seemed greener and more pleasant to the young English man of letters. Southey stayed in Lisbon with his uncle, the chaplain to the British Factory in the popular residential area of Buenos Ayres. The chaplain's house was perched on the western slopes of the city with commanding views of the river. Nevertheless, despite the comfortable domesticity of his uncle's home and its decent library of books, Southey seems at first to have succumbed to the usual expatriate irritation at the heat and dust of Lisbon. Wherever he went he was assailed by gangs of beggars who stuck as tenaciously to foreigners as the mosquitoes. Church bells pealed out day and night invading his privacy and preventing him from sleeping properly. Nor was the demanding critic impressed by the Portuguese. His innate suspicion of Catholic society was confirmed by learning that the majority of aristocrats did little more than languish their days attending the court, neglecting their estates and all other duties. If they were not a sufficient target, there was always the Inquisition, with its barbaric public burnings in the centre of the city, to rail against. But Southey did not have a low opinion of the Portuguese alone. He rated his fellow countrymen little higher. They had no knowledge of the culture of the country they lived in, preferring to waste their time

at the card tables night after night. His uncle, a fluent Portuguese
speaker, was a noble exception.

Occasionally Southey was impressed by someone whom he met.
The Italian poet Angelo Talassi was a guest at his uncle's house and
entertained the young English man of letters with his improvising
skills. Contact of that sort contrasted favourably with the culture-
less activities of the expatriate community. There were also parts
of the city to be enjoyed. He particularly liked the narrow, twisted
streets of the Alfama. Outside of the city, the wild, rugged slopes
of the Sintra mountain were a source of inspiration.

By the time Southey returned to Lisbon in 1800 for a second visit
he had started to give the lusophone world serious scholarly attention. He claimed to find both Portuguese and Spanish easy languages
to read and had returned after his first visit with a thorough ground-
ing in both. Now his ambitious plan was to write a monumental work
on the history of Portugal and all her overseas territories. This vast
undertaking would cover many volumes and establish him for good
as the historian of the Lusitanian world, as Gibbon had become
the historian of Rome. Indeed Portugal would provide a modern
example of an imperial power that had flourished and declined,
just as Rome had done. But the grandiose plan never materialized.
A decade later he did produce a history of Brazil in several volumes,
but that was as far as the grand scheme went. The history was only
lukewarmly received. Meanwhile Southey poured scorn on some
of the works on Portuguese themes which were being published in
England. He found W.J. Mickle's translation of Camões's *Lusiads*,
which had appeared in 1776, heavy in style and not close enough
to, nor as elegant as, the original. Even more scathing was his view
of James Murphy's account of his travels in Portugal. Like many
other travel books of the period, Murphy's lacked lustre; it proved
too prosaic for the taste of the poetic Southey.

Southey's literary labours had in fact broken his health, so
he returned to Portugal a sick man, with frayed nerves and a
quirky disposition. This time there was a palpable excitement in

his description of his first sight of Lisbon, with its churches and convents silhouetted against a blue sky and its harbour crammed full of vessels from every corner of the world. Soon he and his wife Edith were ensconced in a house near his uncle's. From the very desk where he wrote he had a fine view of the bustling estuary of the Tagus. With its ships and boats and flags fluttering in the breeze, it was an auspicious vista for a historian of empire to gaze upon when pausing from his serious pursuits.

For a while it seemed that Southey's return to Lisbon had re-invigorated him. His days were spent arranging his papers and planning his research; his evenings were given to intelligent conversation with his uncle, a well-read cleric who had always encouraged his nephew's interest in Portuguese history and culture. Southey was now a good deal more relaxed in his attitude to Catholicism, realizing that the Catholic clergy were among the more cultured members of the local community. Having learnt his lesson from his first visit, he kept away from the English community, annoyed by both the philistines among the Factory members and the aristocracy who came to Lisbon merely to indulge themselves in banquets and celebrations. But his good humour did not last. Working each day in his uncle's well-stocked library, he was plagued by the constant ringing of bells, sometimes in the private chapels of nearby homes. As the city became unbearably hot, he needed a change of scenery and something to inspire him. Sintra provided both. Southey moved to live in his uncle's remote cottage, amid the lemon and orange trees. In that romantic and inspiring landscape of mountain and stream, he passed perhaps the happiest days of his life, sometimes in the company of a Miss Barker rather than his staid wife Edith, wandering the hills and planning his great literary projects. Southey's nostalgia for those days never left him; visiting Lisbon had a lasting effect on his career as a writer, not all of which proved beneficial.

Unlike the learned Southey, Byron arrived in Portugal with little knowledge of the country and even less of the language. He boasted that his Portuguese was confined to swear words, which were enough for him to bear down upon the natives. Yet the poet's first description of Lisbon portrays a majestic city:

> What beauties doth Lisboa first unfold!
> Her image floating on that noble tide,
> Which poets vainly pave with sands of gold[16]

When he was leaving, only two weeks later, he wrote home in a cheerful tone saying that he has been happy eating oranges, talking to monks in bad Latin and swimming the Tagus. Byron and John Cam Hobhouse, who accompanied him, did the tourist rounds with intensity during their short stay. They went to the theatre, visited monasteries and churches, paid a visit to Sintra, and no doubt imbibed a fair measure of Portuguese wine. Both were shocked by the griminess of Lisbon. The wild dogs mentioned by every foreign visitor of the time were bad enough; but tourists were also exposed to being attacked by gangs of youths armed with knives. The mendicant clergy who thronged the streets particularly offended the more puritanical Hobhouse. Unlike Byron, Hobhouse was not amused by their poor command of Latin. Whether Hobhouse's negative views came to influence Byron or whether the poet simply changed his mind, by the time he came to publish *Childe Harold*, three years later in 1812, the relaxed mood of the tourist has completely vanished. Instead, a distinctly lusophobe tone runs right through the work.

Byron and Hobhouse had come to Portugal at a bad time. The country was under threat of French invasion. The Portuguese royal family had fled to Rio de Janeiro accompanied by the British Navy, an apparently supportive gesture from an old ally, which nevertheless protected British economic interests. During the entire period of the French invasions, there was considerable destruction to buildings and much pillaging of works of art and other valuables. Despite finding these grim legacies of French occupation, Byron was still impressed by the scale of Lisbon and enjoyed its environs. He records his pleasure at the polychromal interior of Mafra convent but it was Sintra, particularly with its romantic, almost wild setting, that most appealed to his poetic nature. The frugal monks of Pena convent provided a salutary contrast to the debauched clergy of the city. Gazing at the panorama he is at his most expansive:

> Lo! Cintra's glorious Eden intervenes
> In variegated maze of mount and glen.
> Ah me! what hand can pencil guide, or pen,
> To follow half on which the eye dilates
> Through views more dazzling unto mortal ken
> Than those whereof such things the bard relates,
> Who to the awe struck world unlock'd Elysium's gates?[17]

Byron loved every aspect of Sintra, even the 'fairy dwelling' ruin of William Beckford at Monserrate, where he finds something gothic and even ghostly in the air. Here amid the grandeur of nature is also to be found the dark and sinister forces that drive man to doom and destruction. It has to be the starting point for Childe Harold's pilgrimage, a spiritual as much as a physical journey through adversity and harshness as well as grandeur and nobility. One of the places that Childe Harold passes is the site of Seteais Palace, one of the Marialva homes, where Byron mistakenly thought the Convention of Cintra had been signed the year before, in 1808.[18]

By the terms of the Convention, the French General Junot was allowed to leave the country with his army's booty intact. No reparations to compensate for the enormous damage to Portugal were written into the armistice agreement which the British commander-in-chief, Sir Hugh Dalrymple, had concluded at nearby Torres Vedras, the site of Wellington's later entrenchments. The French negotiator, Marshall Kellerman, must have been delighted with the terms of the peace settlement. Although Dalrymple may have been taking a practical view that the terms would be accepted without more bloodshed, it was a bad settlement for Portugal, leaving the country weak and at the mercy of the British, something which, if not the covert objective of British policy, nevertheless did British interests no harm.

Byron did not seem to accept that the armistice had been unfairly foisted on Portugal when its leaders had little choice but to acquiesce. He took the rather ungenerous view that the Portuguese had been craven to agree to such conditions without a fight. Although the English press had at first taken the view that the settlement was probably sensible given the strength of the French bargaining position, opinion soon swung the other way and the Convention was attacked as a national disgrace. Eminent subjects of the crown, including William Wordsworth, wrote tracts and verse deploring what had happened; Beckford and Southey were shocked by its terms. While some critics, like Sir Walter Scott, claimed that the settlement would not have happened if Sir Arthur Wellesley (later Duke of Wellington) had been in command instead of Dalrymple, others blamed it on the great man himself. No decent Englishman could accept that the old ally had been well served.

Brooding on these sinister matters, Childe Harold blames the Portuguese for lacking the spirit to fight for freedom. Byron's strong lusophobic remarks have attracted much attention and rebuttal from Portuguese scholars and critics over the ages. Francisco Costa ascribed the poet's utterance to a malevolent streak in him; others have insisted that Byron was caught up in a matrimonial tangle having made advances to a married woman. His public humiliation – of being slapped in public outside a Lisbon theatre – implanted in him a need for revenge.[19] Byron's own explanation is given in a hidden footnote to *Childe Harold*. He says:

> As I found the Portuguese, so I have characterised them. That they have since improved, at least in courage, is evident. The late exploits of Lord Wellington have effaced the follies of Cintra, changed the character of a nation, reconciled rival superstitions, and baffled an enemy, who never retreated before his predecessors.[20]

So Byron had taken against the Portuguese because of what he perceived to be their lack of martial spirit. It was only when led by an English commander that they had begun to stand their ground against the French. Although this is a harsh judgement against a small nation attacked by the strongest European power of the day at a time when its ablest leaders had fled abroad, it would have been an opinion shared by many Englishmen who experienced the Peninsular Wars. Byron was a young man imbued with ideas of glorious struggles for freedom: it was the stuff of heroes; an excited call to arms. The absence of a fighting spirit in any nation would have attracted his scorn. Byron's attitude towards Portugal was therefore a complex one. He made up his mind early on that the Portuguese were a servile race. They hardly deserved to have the paradise of Sintra as their own. Ironically, Byron's romantic evocation of Sintra and the legend of *Childe Harold* had a profound effect on the imagination of both the English and the Portuguese long after his calumnies were forgotten.

Although Byron's reference to Wellington as the English general who stiffened up the Portuguese, it was Marshall William Carr Beresford who in fact took control of the Portuguese army as its commander-in-chief in 1809. The British had been deeply involved in Portuguese affairs since the evacuation of the royal family to Brazil two years before; leading military figures left the country with the king, and the subsequent French invasion left the Portuguese army totally demoralized. Beresford was determined to restore discipline in its ranks; he deployed British officers across its entire structure. Although Beresford's suzerainty was acceptable enough during the campaigns against the French – he received a Portuguese baronetcy in recognition of his services in 1810 – his continued presence after the war had ended was less welcomed. As a favourite of the absent king, he was a political force equal to the rump of ministers who retained nominal control; he soon became known as the odious Briton who interfered in everything, including the conduct of

civil administration, something unforgivable to the remaining
Portuguese courtiers.

In 1815 Beresford went to Brazil to re-establish his credentials
with the king personally. It was an astute move for he returned to
Lisbon as marshall general of all the king's armies with a mandate
to reform them as he wished. Beresford lived in some style at the
Palace of Junqueira, becoming amorously involved with the Viscon-
dessa de Juromenha, wife of the Visconde. As viceroy, Beresford
was effectively dictator; his stern manner did nothing to placate
fractured Portuguese sensibilities. In 1817 there was an alleged
conspiracy against the crown led by General Gomes Freire de
Andrade but it may have been directed against Beresford as much
as the king. The British commander-in-chief used intelligence
methods to infiltrate the group; in due course the conspirators were
ruthlessly executed by the Portuguese authorities on his advice;
the leader himself was executed in prison. Beresford's role in the
conspiracy renewed the campaign against him.[21] He once more
made for Brazil to get further support from the king and once
again he managed to get royal approval for his continuing role.

By the time he returned to Europe in 1820, the Liberal Constitutionalists had taken control and Beresford was prevented from
returning to Lisbon. It was only with the restoration of the monarchy that the position changed once more and Beresford was able
to return to Lisbon in 1823. But his time was up, the Machiavellian
moment had passed and he could no longer influence the course of
events. Neither then nor in 1826 on another visit did he manage
to re-establish himself in his once overpowering position.

One literary tourist of the eighteenth century who had strong
links with England but was not himself British was Giuseppe
Baretti, the Italian man of letters who had been well received
by Dr Johnson and other members of the Literary Club when he
took up residence in London in 1751. His Portuguese recollections
originally contained comments critical of the Portuguese government and had to be revised to soothe ruffled Iberian sensibilities.

He came to Lisbon in 1760, only five years after the earthquake, staying like so many foreigners in the Buenos Ayres district to the west of the centre of the city. Baretti was obviously shocked at what he saw: large parts of the city still lay in ruins; rebuilding was under way but at a slow pace. Like so many other visitors, he complains of the unsightly piles of rubbish dumped in the streets, the roaming wild dogs and the general dilapidation of the buildings that had actually survived the tremors and the floods of 1755. His description of a ravaged city, full of pickpockets, dwarf-like inhabitants and plump middle-class gentlemen who were 'not melted into slenderness'[22] borders on the picaresque.

Even so, Baretti did not underestimate the task facing the authorities and the citizens. He understood that many Lisbon folk had lost everything – possessions, homes and businesses from which to make a living. Being a practical man, he observed that even the tools needed to rebuild houses were lacking since they too had been swept away by the earthquake and its after-math. His real criticism was of the direction being taken in the reconstruction. Instead of concentrating on what was for him the most important thing – rehousing the inhabitants – huge effort was invested in the building of a grand new arsenal. With some incredulity, Baretti himself witnessed the scene of the laying of the foundation stone of this structure. Procession after procession of grandees arrived in coaches. First came the patriarch in a gilt coach lined with blue velvet and escorted by a further seven coaches with any number of liveried attendants. Next came Prime Minister Pombal's entourage, which was followed by the royal party in many more coaches (Baretti notices the Irish, Scots and German attendants in this posse). Despite the sweltering heat of an early September day the great and good had turned up for the ceremony in force. It lasted for more than an hour and left the attendees exhausted.[23]

Baretti much enjoyed the hills and dales in which Lisbon was built. He greatly admired the elegance of the aqueduct, which once

seen cannot be forgotten, and the fine views across the Tagus to
Almada nestling on the other side.[24] The monastery of Jerónimos
impresses him for its scale and the commodious accommodation of
the monks. Sintra casts its usual, poetical spell on the visitor. But
these observations are less acute than Baretti's understanding of
what makes the city tick. One of its most prominent social features
is its mixture of races: black, Jewish and Arabic mixed with various
Caucasian strains. He remarks that 'with such a variety of odd
faces' the traveller must doubt 'whether Lisbon is in Europe' and
he speculates on the possibility of a future when there would be
no 'pure' Portuguese living in its surrounds.[25]

One of Southey's 'Goths' (northerners whom he deemed to
be of the right sensibility to enjoy the South) to visit the city a
generation after Baretti was the botanist M. Link. Link, a university professor and established writer, came with the Count de
Hoffmannseg in 1797, the year before Beckford's last visit. The
two tourists covered the entire length of the country from north
to south. Link's scientific interest was much stimulated; he identified numerous plants which had thitherto been uncategorized or
unrecorded. But his interest was not confined to botanical matters; he was an acute observer of Portuguese society and culture
in the widest sense. There is a great deal of social and economic
data in his account – details of agricultural production and the
commercial trading activities of Lisbon come under his intense
scrutiny. He was particularly concerned with trying to analyse
the causes of Portuguese economic decline during the course
of the century. But he also wanted to enjoy cultural aspects of
Portuguese life, visiting the theatre and listening to music. His
collected works on travel, including the Portuguese episode,
gained wide attention and was admired by Goethe and Schiller
among others.[26]

Nearly a century later another northern man of letters, much
better known than Link, arrived in Lisbon in 1866, taking up
residence with the Danish ambassador. This was Hans Christian

Andersen, who stayed in Pinheiros, to the west of the city, not far from the place where Baretti had stayed before him. Hans Christian Andersen gives an enthusiastic account of the bucolic hills of that part of Lisbon:

> Late in May the hills are still green, as at home in Denmark. Little fields of maize peep out between the *quintas*, the name used for a house and garden in the country. Olive trees all round amid the corn; the feeling of fruitfulness and freshness and the abundance of the trees remind me of Kent. To the west the hills on the horizon are literally sown with small windmills, one after another, like a line of battlements.[27]

In one direction he sees the 'dizzying' arches of the aqueduct and beyond the hidden gardens of Lisbon. In the other Sintra broods in the clouds. Like Baretti, Hans Christian Andersen is mesmerized by the aqueduct, towering over everything and reducing all other structures to insignificance. In nearby Laranjeiros, in the grounds of the *quinta* of Baron Quintela, he is delighted to find a theatre hidden amid greenhouses and Chinese pavilions. The estate itself is somewhat derelict, adding a romantic charm familiar to Lisbon houses through the ages. A more lively contrast is provided in the nearby mansion of the Marquis of Fronteira, where Italianate terraces and Roman busts lend a classical feeling that is nonetheless made exotic by Eastern willows and hidden grottoes.

In contrast to many other visitors, Hans Christian Andersen does not find the streets of Lisbon itself dirty or disagreeable. He described broad, well-kept avenues and handsome villas with tiled fronts. The main theatre (Queen Maria II) is imposing while the Baixa, with its gleaming and well-lit jewellers' shops, could be in Genoa or Edinburgh on account of a similar grid system. One interesting literary encounter he has is with António Feliciano de Castilho, though blinded in his youth an avid enthusiast for classical literature.[28] Castilho was married to a Danish lady, Froken Vidal, and had learnt his wife's language. This greatly eased contact between the two literary men. When they met, Hans Christian

Andersen found the Portuguese writer busy on a translation of Virgil. Later they entered a literary correspondence, in Danish on the one side and in French on the other, just one more symbol of the continuing foreign presence in the city.

6

From Royal to Republican City

Dona Maria II ascended the throne in 1834 after a decade of strife and civil war. The queen had been born in Rio de Janeiro in 1819 towards the end of the long period of the exiled court. That exile had begun in 1807 when Dom João (the queen's grandfather), as prince regent, had at last been persuaded by the British to leave Portugal as the French armies invaded the country. Dom João had gone to Rio with the two young princes, Dom Pedro (the Queen's father) and Dom Miguel (her uncle). Both boys spent their formative years in the 'tropical Versailles',[1] where the court remained for more than a decade. When Dom João (as king) finally returned to Lisbon in 1821 to face demands for a constitutional monarchy, Dom Pedro remained in Brazil, making his famous declaration of independence, 'Independence or Death', in 1822 and installing himself as emperor.

When Dom João died in 1826, Dom Pedro succeeded to the throne of Portugal. Intending to remain in Brazil, he named Maria as regent in Portugal. However, within a short time, his brother Dom Miguel returned to Portugal. Making it clear that he would have no truck with liberal constitutionalism, Dom Miguel declared himself king. His move forced Dom Pedro to return to Portugal and the struggle between the princes (known as the war of the two brothers) lasted for six years, culminating in Dom Miguel's defeat at Evoramonte in 1834. Under the terms of the settlement, Dona Maria would marry her uncle (a not uncommon Bragança arrangement), leaving Dom Pedro free to return to Brazil. The marriage never took place; instead Dom Miguel went into exile in Germany refusing to renounce his claim to the throne.

These were not propitious circumstances for the ascent of a 15-year-old princess to the throne. Fundamental disagreement about the role of the monarch continued to undermine political stability. When Dom Pedro had first installed Maria as regent, he had done so on the basis of the 'Charter', a constitutional settlement under which the monarch remained a strong figure. Certain restraints on the activity of the crown – for example, having to heed the opinion of parliament – were concessions from the monarch rather than conditions imposed upon him. In the meantime the economic situation was bad – years of civil strife had left an already weakened commerce in a worse state. In a desperate attempt to bolster the state's own finances, the religious orders were suppressed and a vast amount of church property was seized in 1834. In 1836 a radical movement, intent on destroying the Charter, succeeded in toppling the government (in the so-called September Revolution). The Charter was suspended and a dictatorial government under Manuel Passos ruled without any check until a new constitution was promulgated in 1838. This new constitution, a compromise between systems of absolutist and constitutional monarchy, lasted for four years, giving a much needed breathing space during which there was some economic recovery, evidenced by a growing middle-class way of life in Lisbon.

In the meantime the young queen had been married twice. Her first marriage was to Augustus de Leuchtenberg, who died soon after the marriage; her second was to Ferdinand of Saxe-Coburg, which took place in 1836. When the young Ferdinand arrived in Portugal he was a dashing, if inexperienced, youth of nineteen.[2] At a later date, writing home to his uncle Ernestus I about the impending marriage of his younger brother Leopold to the daughter of the Spanish king, Dom Fernando (as he was always known in Portugal) says that Leopold will need a strong sense of duty to guide him and perhaps the helping hand of an older relative to temper his youthful inexperience. He may well have been reflecting on his own experiences when expressing that opinion about his brother's prospects.[3]

Dom Fernando's own seriousness of purpose and devotion to his adopted country have been obscured by a number of factors, not least of which was his reputation for being a dandy and a lover of the arts. The sobriquet 'the artist king' by which he became known was not meant to be entirely flattering, suggesting as it did devotion to bohemian pastimes rather than to the affairs of state.[4] In fact, deep though his interest in the arts was – Fernando was to make a significant contribution to appreciation and conservation of the national architectural heritage – the royal consort also understood only too well the complexity of the Portuguese political landscape with its many antagonistic factions. As a foreigner, even one who had mastered the language, he had to tread carefully; his sensitivity to the nuances of political life made him anxious not to offend any of the rival groups.

From his first contact with Portuguese society, Dom Fernando lamented what he saw as a lack of social responsibility in its ruling class. Instead of acting together in the national interest and supporting important reforms, such as those in the field of education, which the queen was anxious to introduce, the aristocratic court circle devoted all its energies to plots and to intrigues. This style of court politics had no appeal for the emerging Lisbon middle class of the 1830s. Excluded from the sphere of patrician politics surrounding the monarch, they became more radical. Fernando understood what was happening but it was difficult for him to do much about it. In letters home, he laments the self-destructive quality of the upper class, which will make it difficult for Portugal to progress despite its strategic location on the Atlantic and its benign climate. These problems of governance were exacerbated by a lack of familiarity with or a desire for constitutional monarchy. Portuguese kings had always ruled in an absolutist way. It was only when João VI had had to make concessions to the demands of liberal constitutionalists after the events of 1820 that the absolutist style of governance was challenged. Even then constitutional monarchy was an innovation which had never been welcome by the conservative *fidalgo* families.

Ironically, with his lack of interest in military affairs and his devotion to the arts, Dom Fernando was in fact the perfect constitutional monarch, presiding over the affairs of state but not wishing to direct them. His determination to keep above party strife was another admirable qualification, but it was misunderstood to amount to a detachment and even disinterest in public affairs. His own personal views changed over time; beginning as a conservative, he gradually mellowed into a liberal, concerned with individual freedom and the right of free expression. But Dom Fernando's patriotism remained paramount. He was first offered the crown of Spain, which he rejected having learnt enough about Iberian politics to understand that a reunification of the two countries would be a monumental political blunder. Next came an offer of the Greek throne, which he also turned down.

Instead of intervening in political discussion, Dom Fernando took up the important task of restoring national buildings, some like the Tower of Belém significant symbols of nationhood. At the time when he started to plan the building of Pena Palace in his beloved Sintra, a new consciousness about the national heritage was being born. Dom Fernando was much taken by a coterie of liberal friends – including the writer and critic Alexandre Herculano[5] and Francisco Adolfo Varnhagen (a Luso-Brazilian interested in all aspects of cultural life). Together they persuaded him that the style of architecture at the time of Manuel I in the sixteenth century was the true national style. 'Manuelino' (the term was coined by Varnhagen) was an evolution in Gothic, with florid maritime and oriental touches, such as are found at Tomar and at the Tower of Belém. When Dom Fernando instructed the German architect Ludwig Wilhelm, Baron von Eschwege, he had decided to create a spectacular and exotic building which would crown the Sintra peaks and be visible from miles around.

The building of the palace, on the very steep slopes of the granite mountain, was a considerable engineering challenge but one which the baron, who had already published a detailed geological treatise on Sintra, was well up to. He concentrated on erecting a sturdy medieval-looking castle that borrowed from the German romantic schloss, while the king continued to pay personal attention to the interiors where he created a mixture of medieval, oriental and arabesque rooms. Two ornamental turrets at the main gateway to the palace imitate the Tower of Belém lying on the Tagus estuary. One of the most dramatic features of the façade is the Triton portico. The arch is held up by a giant Triton, carved from stone, who bears the weight of the world on his shoulders. The elaborate twists of rope and maritime images on this massive piece of masonry reflect the great Manueline window at Tomar. Meanwhile, outside in the extensive grounds, Dom Fernando planted a large variety of exotic trees and plants, which had been imported from all over the world. Influenced by English ideas of landscape gardening (and by the particular example of Sir Francis Cook at nearby Monserrate), he aimed to create a 'natural' feeling to the park. The forest would provide a primitive cloak around the castle; clearings for fountains and some pavilions would be scattered here and there to add a feeling of man's presence amid nature. Bridges, grottoes and pergolas gave the grounds a romantic and mysterious atmosphere.

Dom Fernando was a keen family man who enjoyed the bucolic life of a country gentleman, and was interested in the arts, which he encouraged in his own family.[6] He gradually became more reclusive, spending happy days in Sintra with his second wife, Elisa Hensler, a singer of international renown, who became the Condessa d'Edla. But the Lisbon courtiers did not share these delights in quiet country living; nor did they approve of the countess. Although the king continued to attend to his public duties, his gradual withdrawal from court life left a question mark over the role of the monarch. The king was no longer seen as the prime political player, but at the same time the role of a constitutional monarch was not widely accepted as a substitute. A vacuum was being created in the public arena, which was filled by an aspiring middle class whose political proclivity was increasingly republican.

The political background against which this incipient republicanism was emerging was complex. The pattern for almost the entire period was an alternation of conservative and liberal governments, often intent on reversing the policies of their immediate predecessors. The Charter remained a point of reference in these divisive and economically debilitating conflicts. In the early part of the reign, António Bernardo da Costa Cabral emerged as the principal defender of the Charter. Although he believed in strong government, Cabral was also intent on driving through a programme of reform. His measures covered many areas, including the reorganization of the judiciary, further centralization of public services, the construction of roads and bridges and the erection of impressive public monuments such as the national theatre of Maria II in its commanding position in Rossio Square. Cabral's authoritarian style led to a challenge from the liberals, organized in two identifiable groups, the Regenerators on the one hand and the Historicals on the other. Both claimed to champion reform, until the formation of the Progressive Party, under Anselmo Braancamp, assumed the modernizing mantle. These parties alternated in government until the end of the century, providing some measure of stability and a period when the country could recover ground lost earlier in the century.

During this period the city of Lisbon was expanding beyond its old central areas of the Baixa near the river, the Bairro Alto or high quarter on the slopes to the west, and the Moorish Alfama clinging around the castle walls. While new features of development included the laying down of a water system (marked by fountains) as early as the 1820s, other features of the city still retained something of a medieval feel. Small industries, such as the ceramics factory at the Largo do Intendente (named after Pina Manique) called the Fabrica de Cerâmica Viúva Lamego, were still being set up in the very heart of the old centre. The factory was founded in 1849, replacing one in the Rato, and its entrance was marked by a ceramic tableau depicting a Chinese mandarin holding a scroll showing the date of the foundation of the factory. More conventional decorations, depicting industry and commerce (including Mercury, its god), are found inside the building in more elaborate traditional *azulejo* style. But alongside buildings like the factory, other features of the city harked back to a more rural Lisbon of agriculture and the cultivation of fruits. Gardens and orchards remained hidden behind the façades. The names of some of them – like that of the Rua da Horta Seca (literally 'the street of the dry kitchen garden'), running along from the Praça Luís de Camões – were reminders of that association.

This mixture of rural and urban development was much in evidence in the east of the city where the industrial expansion was most pronounced. Proximity to the river and delivery of goods by water were always important considerations; there was now the need to house a growing artisanal and lower middle class around the hills of São Vicente and Graça. In some cases existing structures were used, but in different ways: for example, spacious old clerical buildings were divided up for multiple occupation. Improvised patios and additional outbuildings were added in an unplanned manner, so that the density of population increased significantly in these areas. In some cases, industrial or commercial developers bought up the plots, setting up communities for their workforces to live in. As the suburban sprawl spread further, country houses disappeared and so did the orchards and gardens that surrounded them. The internal courtyards of these houses were built around, with structures rising to three or four levels on all four sides. Whole communities were sheltered from outside in this way. Some of these patio developments are grander than others. Close to Graça is the Vila Sousa, which one enters through a great arch, with cobbled stones in the open space and an ancient lamp post. The interior space is large, the size of a public square, and contains a range of accommodation, ateliers mixed together with larger apartments. The medieval atmosphere of this community is added to by its proximity to the church, with its tradition of religious processions carried on from earliest times. In this case the association is quite specific – at the hermitage of Nossa Senhora do Monte, built after the earthquake of 1755, the stone chair of São Gens, first bishop of Lisbon, is said to have miraculous properties.

One gradual improvement in civic life during the nineteenth century was the provision of better security. Almost all foreign visitors to Lisbon in earlier times had commented on its law-lessness. Brigands and robbers roamed the city streets attacking people at will and destroying property. No one could be sure of ever finishing a journey without some form of challenge or danger. The gangs of bandits sometimes disguised themselves as military personnel so that it was difficult to distinguish them from the law-enforcing authorities. Pombal was well aware of the destabilizing effect this had on commerce He appointed Pina Manique as *intendente* or police chief with a mandate to get to grips with crime and disorder.[7]

Pina Manique was determined to implement policies that would guarantee safe passage to citizens and foreigners going about their lawful business. His first priority was to reorganize the law-enforcing authorities into a more efficient structure. He established thirteen patrols, one for each district of the city. The patrols consisted of 9 horsemen and 15 footmen. In 1801 a distinct force, the Guarda Civil, was separated from the military and took over responsibility for public order in the city. The new force was supported by a local militia, which acted as reinforcements in particularly difficult situations. At the same time the law was tightened up. The carrying of dangerous weapons – such as cudgels, lances and spears – was banned. Gradually even the most notoriously crime-ridden parts of the city, such as the Moorish quarter, were brought under control. Citizens began to realize the benefits of the new measures and supported them. Occasionally harsher action had to be taken. In 1808, during the somewhat paranoid French period, Intendente Lagarde raided various houses suspected of being centres of criminal activity, confiscating property and even expelling individuals from the city or, in the case of foreigners, deporting them.

Despite the political upheavals of the early years of Queen Maria's reign, the life of high society continued unabated. The most vivid guide to Lisbon life during this period is the journalist and essayist Pinto de Carvalho (known as 'Tinop'), whose graphic descriptions bring to life every level of society from the aristocratic salons to the bohemian cafés and drinking houses.[8] Tinop's accounts emphasize the extravagant, epicurean life of high society whose members were devoted to equestrian sports (including bullfighting, where horsemanship was prominent), lavish balls or soirées in their palatial town houses or country manors (*quintas*). Some of these events, such as a party held in 1865 by the Count of Penafiel, could be very grandiose affairs, with as many as fifteen hundred guests attired in the latest fashions coming from Paris and London. Other parties were entirely in fancy dress with different themes to match the seasons. Balls took place in sumptuous apartments, choking with ornate furniture, gilt mirrors and antique furniture (which, in the case of the Count of Penafiel, included a clock that had been made for the Empress Eugénie). Crystal chandeliers, rare bohemian glass and the finest wines added to the luxury; parties went on until dawn, with live orchestras playing all night.

Tinop's *tableau vivant* of the life of high society was meant to titillate and impress a middle-class readership hankering for the grandeur of a more spacious age. But to counterbalance the notion that this was all sheer indulgence, Tinop reminds his readers that the artistic life of the city was also kept alive by this same class of *bon viveurs*. In his elegant *quinta* at Laranjeiras, adorned with classical bronze statues and Reynolds paintings, the second Baron Quintela e Farrobo set up a private opera with a repertoire that rivalled the opera at São Carlos in the city. No doubt the same audience appeared at both venues. By 1830 the Baron had installed electricity at his estate, among other reasons, to improve lighting at his theatrical productions. By doing so he beat the authorities of Lisbon by 20 years.

These stately extravagances were matched by exciting bullfights held at the city bullring. Aristocrats, such as João de Meneses and José Vaz de Carvalho, seemed to be reliving the exploits of their illustrious ancestors on a more domestic scale. They are described as having heroic stature: Meneses has a 'volcanic, Peninsular temperament' and in appearance is like an ancient Roman hero.[9] Carvalho is a ladies' man who thinks nothing of challenging opponents to a duel. Prowess in the equestrian arts remained a sought-after quality in these latter-day knightly heroes.

This aristocratic high life was matched by the less flamboyant pleasures of bourgeois living which were spreading throughout the city. Cafés and taverns were springing up everywhere; *fado* (folk music) and guitar playing could be heard in many venues; exotic Eastern products, such as tea, became widely available to middle-class Lisbonites. Although Pombal had recognized the importance of meeting places where business could be conducted in some comfort, the cafés were regarded with suspicion by Pina Manique who saw them as potential centres of political unrest. The fact that cafés had a Parisian origin, with revolutionary undertones, did not help to dispel this suspicion. During the Napoleonic years which followed, all things with a French connection became odious to the Portuguese. However, Tinop treats the subject of this association with irony; while he notes that Lisbon cafés exist, as their French counterparts, to provide comfort and refreshment, he doubts that there is any intellectual tradition of the sort that would fuel opposition politics in them. Even the London clubs were more likely to be hotbeds of dissent.[10]

The earliest cafés seem to have come into being a decade or so before the earthquake of 1755, although taverns selling liquor had existed much earlier. The Rose café already existed in the 1740s and was situated in the Rua Nova (later the Rua dos Capelistas). It was frequented by foreigners as well as locals. Another venue for the foreign community was Madam Spencer's in Santa Catarina, where meals and musical entertainment were provided. These venues would have received a boost from the expansion of commercial business which accompanied Pombal's rebuilding of the city after 1755. By the early nineteenth century there had been a proliferation of such outlets. One of these was run by a Marcos Filipe in the Largo do Pelourinho, where tea and a special buttered toast (a version of which survives as a much favoured snack to modern times) were served.[11] This *botequim* was popular with Lisbonites as well as foreigners; no doubt the generous portions of a home-made liquor helped to add to its popularity.[12] Business in this establishment was so good that the owner was able to contribute to the rehabilitation of ex-soldiers after the French withdrawal. Several decades later, the tavern did become a centre for radical politics. A group called the Arsenalistas (who first met at the naval arsenal) gathered there in 1838 to protest against the new constitution of that time.

Another establishment, which attracted the attention of the authorities, was the café O Greco ('The Greek'), which took its name from its owner, one Angiolo Canalhoti. It was known to be a meeting place for radicals even at the time of the French occupation, and never entirely lost that reputation afterwards. The clientele were a mix of locals and foreigners. Some of them were distinguished by their unusual dress and appearance. One of them, Pedro Candido, is described as a 53-year-old, tall, thin, of a ruddy complexion, with a crooked nose and small, squinting eyes. He habitually wore black and sported a large-brimmed black hat, giving off a 'revolutionary' image. The owner, Canalhoti, was himself in trouble with the authorities from time to time, on occasion having to disguise himself in order to avoid arrest. Some customers, like the Englishman Walsh, may have frequented the café merely to pick up on the news and gossip; others like a Senhor Sampaio proved to be immensely loyal, managing to put in an appearance at the café over a period of 82 years.

Other establishments specialized in pastry, starting a craze for sweet-tasting snacks which has never left the inhabitants of the city. Some of these – like the pastry shop of Senhor Puchi in the Largo da Santa Justa in the Baixa – were run by Italians and no doubt frequented by members of the influential Italian trading community in the city. Much later the craze for English teashops arose, where delicacies such as scones could be tried out by the ever-curious Lisbonites.

If politics was discussed in the Lisbon cafés it was not at the expense of literature. The best-known café for the literary set was the Nicola,[13] still in existence in Rossio Square although on a different site. It was frequented by writers like Filinto Elísio, priest and scholar, who rebelled against the neoclassical Arcadian movement of which he was once a part.[14] Elísio was hauled before the Inquisition on suspicion of heretical views and eventually had to flee into exile in Holland and eventually in France where he continued to write freely in a pre-Romantic style. His heterodoxy was only undone by Bocage, the greatest satirical poet of the century, who also frequented the Nicola.[15]

Bocage had been in military service in India but had deserted and fled to Macao, in the Far East. Returning to Lisbon in 1790, he too joined the Nova Arcadia, the literary group, which had egalitarian and libertarian leanings. He was expelled from the society and joined instead the Sociedade da Rosa, suspected of harbouring revolutionary views by Pina Manique. Bocage came to the café with his intimate companion José Agostinho de Macedo, a former Augustinian priest, who, among other charges, is said to have robbed the bookshop of the Paulistas where he had been a reclusive scholar. Tinop described Agostinho as a totally undisciplined and incorrigible character who would accost acquaintances for favours either at the Nicola or outside theatres in Lisbon. Bocage himself took to a bohemian and decadent life with a vengeance, dressing eccentrically and extravagantly and chain-smoking in the café, where, surrounded by acolytes, he improvised verse. Some of the improvising sessions in the Nicola were widely celebrated in literary circles. On one such occasion a contest took place between Bocage and Nicolau Tolentino, a fellow satirical poet.[16] It ended with Bocage hissing out the line that a haphazard poet is a fool without fortune.

It is hardly surprising that the antics of the habitués of the Nicola (among whom was Joaquim Manuel, the Brazilian mulatto and master of the viola and the sad cadences of the languid folk song or *modinha* of his homeland) should have been the subject of a play called the *Casa de Café e Bilhar*, which was set to music by Marcos Portugal. Agostinho, given to outbursts and tantrums, is represented by the character of Lagosta; even the owner of the café, José Pedro dos Lumiares, is satirized. Bocage meanwhile, expelled from the Nova Arcadia, had also been found guilty of seditious writing contrary to religion by the Inquisition and ended his days eking out a living from translations of French literature. Appropriately his funeral costs were paid for by the same owner of the Nicola.

During the French occupation the Nicola became the haunt of officers of the First Empire, in their glittering uniforms, seeking diversion from their duties and entertainment. Their departure in 1808, after the signing of the Convention of Cintra, was marked by a great party at the café. While fireworks burst out all over the city celebrating the liberation of Lisbon by the British, the Nicola had its own celebrations. Lanterns were lit; verses, which had been written by Bocage in the café, were recited. It seemed that the past, sometimes bohemian, character of the place had been vindicated. But this period of grace was not to last. The first Nicola managed to survive until 1834, although after the Napoleonic period its habitués were once again the object of suspicion on the part of the authorities. A succession of cafés with the same name succeeded it in Rossio Square, where the modern, art deco establishment of that name is still to be found.

The cafés of Lisbon, with their sometimes subversive political life, were located in and around the Chiado, which had long been a centre of intellectual activity.[17] In the Trindade the Jesuits had been entrenched for a long time, devising theological and educational policy. Printing presses and booksellers had established trades in the area. During the nineteenth century a number of new theatres and several major newspapers operated within its boundaries. Something of the demi-monde atmosphere of this world is captured by Ramalho Ortigão in his work *As Farpas* (1873), written in collaboration with Eça, in which Portuguese society is satirized.

In 1846 Almeida Garrett and Alexandre Herculano founded the Literary Club (Grémio Literário). Its elegant salons became the refuge of the intellectual elite of the city, whether they were members of the professions (including politicians and public servants), journalists or practising artist and writers. Garrett was himself an heir to the café literature of Bocage and Filinto Elísio; the tradition passed on to Eça de Queirós, who became a habitué of the Club in his early years as a novelist and diplomat. The activities of the Club were widely reported by its journalist members to culturally ambitious members of the growing middle class who did not have entrée to the dazzling world of the intellectual elite.

João Baptista da Silva Leitão Almeida Garrett was born in Oporto in 1799. His childhood was spent partly in the Azores, where his uncle was Bishop of Angra. Garrett showed a precocious interest in all speculative studies whether of a logical or artistic nature. He arrived, full of serious thoughts and a deep religious conviction, at Coimbra in 1816. His days at the university proved formative; in the heady years leading up to the revolt in Oporto in 1819, radical ideas were much in the air. The budding young poet was soon captivated by them. The liberal cause that he was being drawn into had a distinctly anti-clerical tone to it, something that naturally had not recommended it to Garrett's uncle, the bishop. For the young Garrett the new politics also led to a redefinition of religious belief, which now needed to be separated from its institutional base. In the meantime, with conservative opinion dominating the Portuguese court, Garrett went abroad, joining the intellectual expatriate community (*os exilados*) in Paris and later in London.[18]

In Paris Garrett's literary talents began to find serious expression. He wrote two important poems, *Camões* (1825) and *Dona Branca* (1826), while he was in Paris. Distance increased Garrett's nostalgia for his homeland: *Camões* is imbued with a deep sense of *saudades* or feeling of loss of homeland and friends. The poet dwells on sensual memories – the verdant glens and glades of Sintra are given Arcadian clothing; the pastoral peace of the Portuguese countryside is contrasted with the urban life of metropolitan France, a theme later taken up by Eça de Queirós.[19] Without putting aside his religious belief, Garrett was now giving it a humanistic wrapping that derived from Rousseau's belief in the natural goodness of man as well as in the voluptuous sentimentality of Chateaubriand, whose *Atala* he adapted for the stage. When Garrett did return to Portugal in the 1830s he plunged into Lisbon public life with energy, trying to put in place a programme of educational reform which would open up opportunities to a larger section of society. He was at the same time appointed Inspector General of the national theatre, eventually inspiring the building of the new theatre of D. Maria II in its commanding position in

Rossio Square. His passion for the theatre was also evident in his drive to establish proper training for aspirants to the Conservatory of Arts. When the political pendulum swung again to the right, he once again went into exile.[20]

Alexandre Herculano,[21] the co-founder of the Literary Club, came from a less privileged background than Garrett, only gaining financial security on his appointment as royal librarian by Dom Fernando. He was born in 1810, a bleak time in the affairs of Portugal. The French invasion had resulted in considerable physical damage throughout the country; the king and court had moved to Brazil and the economy was in tatters. Herculano's ambition to go to university had to be put aside on the death of his father, a minor public servant. Instead Herculano had to pursue a more utilitarian course in commerce and administration, which would enable him to gain a public service posting. Meanwhile Herculano pursued his literary interests, at the same time allying himself with the liberal cause in politics. Like Garrett, he was influenced by foreign writers including Chateaubriand and Schiller. He made his entry into the literary salons of Lisbon through his friendship with António Feliciano de Castilho, ten years his senior and already well established in literary circles.[22]

However, Herculano's association with the liberal faction did him no good in conservative Lisbon; like Garrett, he eventually went into exile. He first went to England, where he did not settle down well. However, he found his footing in France where the writings of Thiery, Guizot and Hugo widened his horizons further. In 1836 he returned to Portugal, plunging into the intellectual life of Lisbon with zeal. He gained notoriety by attacking conservative governments in press articles. It was only when he was appointed librarian at the royal palaces[23] that he at last gained protection from his enemies as well as financial security. His monumental four-volume *History of Portugal* appeared in 1853. Underlying much of Herculano's writing is an anti-clerical tone; occasionally it came to the surface, for example when he

The Lisbon Aqueduct.
Engraving by G. Vivien, nineteenth century.

Terreiro do Paço.
Painting by D. Stoop, 1662.

The Tower of Belém.

Lisbon Cathedral.

View of the Tagus and Bridge of 25 April.

Ministry of Justice, Praça do Comércio.

View of St George's Castle and Rossio Square.

Monument of the Explorers.
Cottinelli Telmo, 1960.

Marquês de Pombal.
Painting by Louis Michael Van Loo, 1766.

Ruins of St Nicholas Church.
Coloured etching by Jacques Philippe Le Bas, 1757.

Ruins of the Opera House.
Coloured etching by Jacques Philippe Le Bas, 1757.

Marquês de Pombal.
Painting, attrib. J. de Salitre, 1770.

attacked the Office of the Inquisition, which was only finally abolished in 1821.

The literary romanticism of Garrett and Herculano was echoed in the plastic arts. In the 1840s a group of young painters were in revolt against the established Academy, presided over at the time by the conservative figure of André Machado da Cruz. These young artists had imbued the naturalism of Garrett and his insistence, in line with the teaching of Boileau, that the only beauty was to be found in true representation. They were also influenced by the style of a succession of foreign artists who had visited Portugal, particularly the French painter A.J. Noel and the English engraver W.H. Burnett – who in an earlier period had started to produce romanticized views of the Portuguese countryside. One of the leading artists of this school was João Cristino da Silva, who, in 1855, produced his iconic image of *Five Artists in Sintra*, a painting eventually acquired by Dom Fernando. The picture portrays the group[24] in an assortment of dramatic poses, surrounded by curious *saloios* or peasants of the Lisbon area, against the background of hard, granite mountainside. Da Silva uses 'natural' or subdued colours (browns and reds) in the foreground of the painting while providing a dark and grey background by way of contrast. There is a serious mood to the picture which matches the mood of Byron's *Childe Harold*; the eccentric domesticity of the group is contrasted with the somewhat formidable landscape setting. When the five artists were not on one of these country jaunts, they met in Lisbon to complain and conspire against the establishment.

At the time of the publication of Herculano's *History*, José Maria Eça de Queirós was still a schoolboy soon to be heading for Coimbra, like Garret before him. Like Garrett he too imbibed the radical politics of the university, although from his earliest days a satirical inclination was already evident. Eça came from a well-established middle-class background – his father was a judge based in the north of the country. Eça found no difficulty in indulging his penchant for satire of a sometimes acerbic nature

with a professional career in the diplomatic service. Her served in
Cuba and then in England, where he remained for some 14 years.
His last posting was in Paris where he died in 1900. Throughout
this time he wrote about Portugal, in the form of novels, retaining
an objectivity about Lisbon life by being away from it.[25] Unlike
Herculano, Eça took to English society with ease. He adopted the
dress of a dandified English gentleman, which he retained for the
rest of his life. However, he really admired English society because
it seemed to provide freedom for innovation and progress within
the framework of a stable system of governance. Eça observed
bustling Victorian society with approval; he believed that the
energy of the upper classes (which contrasted sharply with the
sloth of their Portuguese counterparts) contributed significantly
to the nation's apparently effortless domination of a large part of
the world.

In France he admired another kind of effortlessness, that of
intellectual liveliness and sophistication. This quality of French
culture, combined with technological advance, contrasted vividly
with the torpor of Portugal. Paris was a glittering city of intellect,
Lisbon a provincial backwater of gluttony. Eça would have agreed
with Alberto Pimentel, an Oporto man who had quipped that
seeing Lisbon was just a preparation for going to Paris.[26] Even so
it is not as simple as that. Eça, ever the satirical moralist, points
out the virtuous benefits of life in a less sophisticated society in
his contrast between metropolitan France and rural Portugal in
The City and the Mountains.[27] However much he shared the liberal
sentiments of his fellow Coimbra radicals like Machado da Rosa,
Eça was above all a satirist who spared no one, whether they were
in or outside the charmed circle of bourgeois life.

Whilst Eça was portraying Lisbon society with satirical preci-
sion from abroad, in the city itself another set of literary men
were solidifying the historic credentials of the city from within.
Julio de Castilho, ensconced in his study in Lumiar, produced a
cascade of books on Lisbon – there were 5 volumes on the old

city, another 12 on the eastern part of it and a further 5 on the riverside. Castilho's method consisted of painstakingly collecting all manner of information on areas, streets and even particular buildings. He read tracts, magazines, journals and newspapers, as well as studying municipal byelaws and official records. From all these sources he gradually amassed a huge and detailed archive on every aspect of civic geography and daily life. The first recognized 'olisipographer', Castilho had many disciples (as we have seen, Tinop was one). Eduardo Freire de Oliveira used his post in the municipal archive to publish a series of works on Lisbon between 1885 and 1911, while the journalist José Joaquim Gomes de Brito worked on his *Ruas de Lisboa*, eventually published posthumously. Later, in the twentieth century, historians like Gustavo Matos Sequeira put the study of Lisbon on a more systematic footing. Castilho's approach was a wide one in which cultural and political history had to be seen as one great tapestry; every aspect of the city's life, including its popular culture, had to be woven into the story. The modern heirs to that tradition continue to produce detailed and at times lavishly illustrated books on every quarter and every aspect of the city.

One writer of the next Lisbon generation who himself stood outside the charmed circle of upper-class Lisbon was Fialho de Almeida, who struggled to make a living from journalism and the writing of short stories.[28] As a medical student, he had begun writing to gain extra income but failed to secure a patron to support him. His idylls of Portuguese rural life way have been deeply felt but his satire of Lisbon society also contained a new, anti-monarchist element. Although, partly as the result of marriage to a wealthy lady, Fialho eventually joined the ranks of the pampered metropolitan literati (assuming the role of a dandy, like Eça) he continued to harbour melancholic thoughts about the lot of man and his place in the order of things.

Fialho saw architecture in ideological terms: schools and public buildings were designed in a distinctly 'nationalistic' style in order to bolster the notion of progress; commercial houses, on the other hand, exuded a confidant opulence in their elaborate façades. Wealthy Brazilians were returning to the city to embellish it with mansions; new avenues radiated out from the centre to stamp the character of bourgeois life on the erstwhile semi-rural ambience of the old suburbs. For Fialho the centre of gravity had moved from the old, aristocratic riverside (with the elaborate and majestic Terreiro do Paço) to the Praça Marquês de Pombal, at the head of a long avenue of mansions and commercial houses. This took the city beyond the old medieval hilltops into new, hitherto semi-rural, areas.

The gentrification of these erstwhile boundary areas of the old city led to a new civic spirit; it echoed the development of Haus-mann's Paris and its mood was similarly republican. As if symbolic of the shift, the marble steps and pier of the old imperial square had been submerged by the river. Sometimes Fialho's survey of Lisbon's monuments takes on a surreal tone, with imaginary structures appearing on the hilltop above the old Moorish castle. Nevertheless there is continuity. Lisbon is a still a vast, commercial emporium: if there is decay around the littoral and a shift towards the hills, the estuary is still the source of much of the city's wealth. But the new sprawl needs a different degree of regulation and planning if the city is to continue to thrive and not become a vast ghost town of empty docks and warehouses by the seashore.

Although the transformation of Lisbon was accelerated in the second part of the nineteenth century, industrialization and urban planning were already under way in the 1830s. The Society for the Promotion of National Industry had been founded in 1822, in rec-ognition of the centralizing of industry and manufacture in Lisbon and Oporto. The Society sponsored a series of modest exhibitions, culminating in the exhibition of 1838. Industrial products were shown off, although the link with agricultural production was not lost. By the time of the 1838 exhibition, a number of significant developments had occurred, including the installation of gas lighting in Lisbon. In 1847 the Companhia Lisbonense de Illuminação a Gas was set up with production facilities right in the middle of town. Many other smaller factories were also located around the littoral so as to benefit from being close to the docks where imported raw materials arrived and from where finished products could be sent away. João Pedro Monteiro began mapping out the industrial areas of the city in a series of lithographs, which show a concentration in areas of Junqueira, Alcântara and Xabregas. During the next decade, the introduction of railways transformed the movement of goods around the country, particularly between the two principal manufacturing bases of Lisbon and Oporto. The location of the rail terminal at Santa Apolónia meant that the eastern section of the city was especially attractive for the location of manufactured goods that would be sent to other parts of the country.

The growth of industries also meant an increase in the working population. Over the whole period the population of the city more than doubled from 160,000 to 400,000.[29] Planning the urban environment became more pressing, with the result that in 1851 a new Ministry of Public Works was set up with a specific remit to oversee urban development. New laws regulating the type of factories that were suited to the city centre were introduced. Factories involved in the production of dangerous substances – such as gunpowder or gas – were relocated to the suburbs. But many other buildings – where a huge range of goods including food (olive oil being especially important), clothing, engineering and marine products, ceramics and even musical instruments – were still being located in the centre.

In 1888 the achievements of this industrial expansion were shown off in a large exhibition. A triumphal gateway, halfway up the new Avenida da Liberdade, symbolized the significance of industrial progress for the economic well-being of the city of Lisbon and the rest of the country.

Pavilions displaying the varied products of manufactories in the capital and elsewhere formed the central buildings of the exhibition. Artists and designers, who had thitherto paid little attention to industrial themes, were commissioned to illustrate and embellish the products of industry and manufacture. Each one of Lisbon's four administrative districts (whose industrial topography was charted in the maps of Isaias Newton) was well represented on particular stands.

The Avenida da Liberdade was itself the grandest of the avenues that emerged as the city spread northwards from the Pombalese Baixa, or riverside. The avenue, which stretched from Rossio to the Praça Marquês de Pombal, was built between 1878 and 1882. The project was not uncontroversial since the new boulevard replaced the old Passeio Público, which had been erected a decade after the earthquake in 1765. The old thoroughfare was an open space; lined with villas and gardens it exuded the grace of an earlier age when the city was still closely tied to its rural hinterland. Along the route were important public buildings such as the Teatro da Rua dos Condes (which was in effect the national theatre) and other palaces and dwellings of the great and good. Although anyone could stroll up and down the 'walk', it was nevertheless conceived as a place of some gentility where ladies and gentlemen dressed properly to parade their status. In some ways the Passeio was a throwback to a pre-commercial Lisbon; an aristocratic society that lived amidst a certain rusticity with links to the countryside rather than to the sea. Overseas trade and commerce, the core of the Manueline city, gradually replaced this older, feudal order, at the same time significantly altering the face of the city. The surviving patrician society nevertheless mingled with the bourgeois citizens of the town: on summer evenings a parade of genteel folk passed up and down its length, latterly illuminated by gaslight.

It is not surprising that the redevelopment of the Passeio became a matter of public controversy. For the modernists, who on this occasion included Fialho de Almeida, it was an important step in raising the status of Lisbon to that of a major European city.

The avenue was the only real boulevard on a Parisian scale to be contemplated in Lisbon. For others, clinging to an older vision of Portuguese society, like the writer Ramalho Ortigão, sweeping away the Passeio was a cutting of the umbilical cord that bound a 'one nation' society, characterized by a kind of feudal classlessness. The traditionalists presented a petition to the crown to preserve the old passage but it proved of no avail: progress swept all aside and the new avenue was inaugurated amid great festivities in 1886 on an occasion that coincided with the marriage of Crown Prince Carlos to Amélia of Orléans.

Once the Avenida da Liberdade was in place, a number of other avenues radiating from it in a northerly and westerly direction were built as the centre of gravity of the city shifted away from the riverside. To the east of the centre, another long thorough-fare, the Avenida Rainha Dona Amélia (later renamed Almirante Reis), ran almost due north towards the area that saw the greatest development in the twentieth century. Along this route blocks of three- and four-storey apartments were erected for the accom-modation of the new bourgeoisie, while to the west the sprawl of older buildings continued. Cafés, tobacconists, barbershops and the ubiquitous *pastelaria* (cake shop) sprang up all over the city. This regeneration breathed life into older industries, such as that of ceramic tiles as the demand for decorative features grew. The traditional blue-and-white motifs gave way to multicoloured tiling effects. At the same time, traditionally aristocratic areas just to the west of the Avenida, in the Bairro Alto, were being modern-ized to provide for more gracious and grander town houses and apartments. A new upper middle class was settling into spacious accommodation around squares such as the Principe Real and in Santa Catarina. Italian influences could be seen in the erection of balustraded balconies and neoclassical window frames in some of the modernized streets. The planting of trees in open spaces and along the avenues gave a protected, shaded feel to the city, particularly welcome in the scorching summers.

Rossio Square itself, the very hub of the city, was also being developed.[30] In its prime location in the vale between the two older hills of the city, Rossio had long been the symbolic as well as geographical centre of the city. At the north end (now the site of the National Theatre) the long façade of the Grand Inquisition Building gave the square a solemn, official look, and in its very centre, the ritual burning of heretics (the *auto-da-fé*) had taken place. Rossio was badly hit by the earthquake of 1755 with the destruction of all its main buildings including the Grand Inquisition headquarters and All Saints Hospital. The square was redesigned on a more strictly geometric pattern by Carlos Mardel as part of the new grid system that emanated from the Praça do Comércio on the riverside. The square resumed its place as the centre of the city and indeed the nation, witness to events such as the French withdrawal in 1808 and the demonstration in favour of the liberal constitution in 1820. A picture of the latter event portrays the allegorical figure of Lisbon (or of Portugal) flying across the square with a banner marked 'Constitution'. In the 1850s the square was transformed once more by the erection of the National Theatre (Donna Maria II), whilst in 1870 the statue of Pedro IV, king and emperor of Brazil was erected amid great pomp and circumstance on a towering plinth where it remains to the present day. Despite these regal and imperial trappings, Rossio remained a square of popular, even rustic, activity. Street entertainers, musicians and vagabonds were always to be found in its precincts; the *saloio* (peasant) character of the hinterland continued to be represented in market stalls where, within living memory, poultry and other country wares continued to be sold. Fruit stalls and flower vendors vied with the sleeker passers-by heading for the new cafés – whether the Suiça on the eastern side of the square or the relocated Nicola on the west. The bustling streets south of the square appealed much to visitors like Thomas Mann.

Certain preoccupations of the *Lisboetas* never seemed to change. By the early nineteenth century, the *fado* or folk song of the city was well established, although there is no consensus about its origin. If the etymology of the word points to Latin (*fatum* or fate) there is no clear link with classical times. Roy Campbell suggested that the first time the word appeared in print was in Brazil in 1810.[31] Some claim a Moorish origin for *fado* which brings with it a deep romanticism; others say that it originated at the time of the discoveries, aboard ship when sailors felt homesick and expressed their feelings in song. Another possible source could be the African slaves on their way to a lifetime exile in Brazil, or Portuguese prisoners destined for a remote part of empire; their laments would have been transmitted back again across the seas to the mother country. Whatever its origin, *fado* is about loss and the lament of loss recalled; it is an expression of the Portuguese notion of *saudades*, that nostalgia which comes from the realiza-tion that was has been lost cannot be regained. In the broadest sense, *fado* fits into the cultural concept of *Sebastianismo*: the grief that accompanies the recollection of irreplaceable loss, of people as well as of place.

Fado is sung by the *fadista*, either a man or woman, accom-panied by two guitars – the Portuguese *guitarra* and what the Portuguese call the Spanish guitar, although originally it was accompanied by the viola. It is usually heard in silence; the lyrics recall the sadness of loss and the pain of those experiencing loss. From the nineteenth century onward, renowned women *fadistas* have dominated the Lisbon *fado* houses. The first of these was Maria Severa Onofriana ('Severa'), who was born in 1820 and sang fados in obscure *tascas* or taverns in the old quarter of the Mouraria. Her bohemian lifestyle was changed when she met the Count of Vimioso, an aristocrat who frequented the *tascas* of the old city. However, the decadent life of the count did not suit Severa, who gave up the relationship and returned to her singing career.

Although *fado* has always had a populist feel to it, it has not been the exclusive preserve of the working classes. Several aristocratic

ladies, among them Barboleta and Scarnidia, the latter rejected
by her family on account of her bohemian proclivities, became
notable *fadistas* They were followed by Custódia and Cesária de
Alcântara. Sometimes the squalid conditions of the singers' lives
– the exploitation, abuse and unwanted children – were reflected in
the words of the song. At different times *fado* was adopted by different political groups. In the 1820s it was associated with liberal,
radical politics; later it was taken up by the socialist movement
and regarded as being proletarian in character. In the twentieth
century, the greatest performing *fadista,* Amália Rodrigues, was
adopted by the Salazar regime as a symbol of patriotic and populist
fervour.

If *fado* has been one enduring staple of popular culture in
Lisbon, another event has been the *festa* or festival, public entertainments usually held out of doors. Like other European entertainments, the Lisbon *festas* were closely associated with religious
celebrations, some of which were based on older pagan rites. The
Christian calendar was replete with saints' days and other feast
days; Saturnalian celebrations could be traced back to Roman
times when the injunction had been to eat, drink and be merry. The
Church reinforced its considerable authority by holding religious
festivities, usually accompanied by symbolic processions. While
these could be glittering and highly theatrical, other festivities
had a more populist feel. This was the case with carnival, the
pagan–Christian celebration of the advent of spring when the
expected natural bounty was anticipated in an orgy of self-in-
dulgence. Carnival was enacted in the streets with considerable
pageantry; it brought people of all backgrounds together and the
outburst of energy led to a renewed civic identity.

One of the most spectacular of Lisbon's festivals centred
round the cult of St Anthony, a figure venerated across the entire
country.[32] As he was a local boy, the municipal authorities took
over honouring the saint so that the Church alone did not retain
a monopoly of the goodwill that the public entertainments en-

gendered. Nevertheless, the celebrations of 13 June (the saint's name day) began with the holding of a solemn Te Deum and pontifical Mass. A grand procession wended its way through the city beginning on the steep slopes near the Cathedral close to St Anthony's birthplace. Lisbonites dressed up in ancient costume; rural semi-pagan features such as the burning of Judas or rural practices such as the burying of *bacalhau* (salted codfish) were added to the entertainments. The popular nature of the festival is indicated by the combination of music, drink and dance that accompanied the feast day. The Praça da Figueira, right in the centre of town, is transformed into a vast fair with stalls selling country products, returning to its original function as the city's market. In other parts of the city, for example in the Campo de Ourique, great gatherings of citizens in traditional dress parade through the square; dancing and marches through the surrounding streets bringing the whole area to life. For many centuries St Anthony had taken his place alongside St Vincent as one of the patron saints of the city.

The importance of public events in Lisbon was understood by the political classes as well as by the Church. Street processions and events were part of the civic life of the city over the ages. In modern times Salazar understood the patriotic impulses that could be harnessed to such events. In 1934 the messianic mission of Portugal towards her colonies was celebrated in a festival of music, folklore and exhibitions designed to tap the reservoir of nationalistic sentiment.

Another popular entertainment encouraged by the authorities was the bullfight and the cult of equestrian display particularly associated with the Portuguese version of the spectacle. The Iberian bullfight can be traced back to Roman times; during the Moorish period when bullfighting continued to flourish, the practice of actually seizing the animal was introduced. Occasions of political importance, such as royal weddings, were celebrated by the staging of bullfights, most spectacularly in the great squares of the city.

One of the most spectacular was staged in the Terreiro do Paço, right outside the royal palace itself. The vast open space would enable a huge crowd, drawn from all sections of society, to gather for the event. Rossio was another favoured venue, adding to the many public events, including the burning of heretics, which have taken place there. It was only in the nineteenth century that arenas dedicated exclusively to bullfighting were introduced – first at the Rua do Salitre near the Passeio Público and later at the modern site of the Campo Pequeno, in the northern extensions of the city. Attempts were made at various times to ban bullfighting altogether. However, its immense public popularity prevented that happening. The only concession that those against what they regarded as a bloody spectacle could gain was to have the bull killed behind the scenes, with the distribution of the carcass to the poor.

Less exotic and more typically European features of Lisbon life were also developing, particularly in the area of transport. Luxurious horse-drawn coaches known as *Americanos* were introduced in the 1870s, although people of modest means still moved around by mule and cart. Railways had gradually linked Lisbon to all the major cities. The Lamanjat line connected the city with Sintra (still a favoured royal residence), although one of its earliest English passengers, Lady Jackson, was unimpressed by the service, complaining about the jolting and the frequency of stops.[33] At the turn of the century electric trams were introduced, becoming one of the best-known symbols of Lisbon daily life. At about the same time, elevators linking lower and higher levels of the hilly city also made their appearance. The most famous of these, with its ornate ironwork, was the Santa Justa, connecting the Baixa with the Bairro Alto. It was in service in 1901, built by Raul Mésnier de Ponsard, a Luso-French disciple of Eiffel, in the same elaborate style as the Paris landmark. The great metal structure towers 136 foot. Ornate cabins with interior woodwork carry passengers up and down the steep sides of the hill. Originally powered by steam, the mechanism was converted to electricity. A series of other elevators operate at precipitous points in the city, the Elevador da Bica connecting the Calçada do Combro and the Rua de São Paulo plunges down sharply and offers dramatic views.

If these various developments were making Lisbon a city fit for the bourgeois to live in; in working-class areas, where accommodation was poor, the first signs of proletarian unrest began to manifest themselves. Mutual Providence societies started to appear in the 1850s, proliferating during the last half of the century until they numbered hundreds of associations with large memberships by the early 1900s. These embryonic socialist organizations were spearheaded by literary intellectuals, notably Antero do Quental and other members of the so-called generation of 70 whose concern extended to the rural as well as the urban poor. Conditions in the countryside were so grim that migration to Brazil continued to increase substantially during this period. At the same time, lack of investment in industry slowed up the economy and had serious effects on urban employment as the population grew. The rotation of political parties in government did little to stem the downward economic trend, fuelling frustration among the working classes and encouraging the formation of more radical, syndicalist organizations on French lines. By 1873 the incipient socialist movement boasted 200 members with its own journal, the *Pensamento Social*. At the same time the Associação Protectora do Trabalho Nacional was founded, bringing together the new left forces on the political landscape. Paul Lafargue, Marx's son-in-law, visited Lisbon to meet José Fontana, the local socialist leader. But the forces of the left did not present a united front. Radical intellectuals, working-class unionists and aspiring socialist politicians juggled for power. While the socialists supported the republicans in the elections of 1899 and 1900, the unions moved to a more extreme, anarchist position inspired by the teaching of Bakunin.

In 1891 a serious republican revolt took place in Lisbon which, in an ominous sign for the monarchy, attracted support from the military. Xenophobic passion had been stirred up by the presentation of the British ultimatum the year before, in which Portugal was curtly informed by its oldest ally that no further attempt to link the African colonies of Angola and Mozambique would be tolerated because it interfered with the north–south African territorial ambitions of Britain. To nationalists across the entire political spectrum, the ultimatum was seen as a humiliating measure of the country's weakness. The ruling classes and the monarchy itself were held responsible for promoting a colonial policy which they could not implement. The discontent that the ultimatum provoked, combined with the continuing economic decline, meant that conditions were ripe for a serious challenge to the entire political order. Cosmetic attempts were made by conservative elements to restore a sense of national pride. A revival of Manueline architecture, notably in Rossio station, was meant to hark back to the golden age, the explorations; a national anthem was composed by Alfredo Keil and celebrations of monarchy and religion took place. However, the tide of republicanism would not be stemmed by these gestures. It became increasingly clear that the monarchy itself was under threat. Repressive measures were taken after the revolt of 1891. Troublemakers were identified and deported; attempts were made to brand the opposition with anti-patriotic colours. Whilst labour was increasingly organized through a series on congresses, characterized by both an anti-clerical and an anti-monarchist stance, a far more radical, anarchist movement began to assert the need for direct action against the bourgeois establishment.

In 1895 the king's carriage was stoned as it was passing through the city. By the time of King Edward VII's visit in 1903,[34] serious strikes became a regular feature of the city's life. Nevertheless the bourgeoisie continued to enjoy the fruits of technological progress. In 1904 the first cinema was opened in Lisbon (O Salão Ideal); telephonic communication with other parts of the country had become possible; electricity was available for domestic use. This comfortable style of life, available only to a few, was protected by strict police vigilance, keeping disturbances away from residential parts of the city. In 1907 a dictatorship under João Franco attempted to wipe out the anarchists without success; republican sentiment was now firmly established and could not be eradicated.

The royal family itself was held together by the strong character of the last queen of Portugal, Amélia, a Norman princess. She preferred the quietness of Sintra to the increasingly disturbing atmosphere of Lisbon. Much of the family life was led there in the lofty palace on Pena peak, built by Dom Fernando. On 2 February 1908, returning from the country, the king and queen drove through the city in an open landau accompanied by their two sons. As the carriage left the Praça do Comércio, republican extremists fired on the royal group, killing the king and the crown prince. The queen and Dom Manuel, the younger son, escaped unharmed. In these highly inauspicious circumstances, Dom Manuel ascended to the throne. Despite the dismissal of the João Franco government, opposition to the monarchy itself continued to mount. On 3 October 1910, a large contingent from the garrison, supported by citizens, declared a republican revolution. When the navy joined them a few day later, it was clear that the days of the monarchy had ended. Dom Manuel abdicated and went into exile in England.[35]

The White City

An unusual and futuristic view of Lisbon was portrayed in a book published in 1906 by Melo de Matos with the deliberately provocative title *Lisboa no anno 2000*. Melo de Matos was an engineer by training; he was a technophile who believed that the rapid progress in technology would transform civic life radically and for the better. In what would be an exciting and startling modernization of the city, Portuguese engineers and scientists would take their place in the vanguard of all the developments that would come about. Melo de Matos's vision was firmly grounded on what had always been the city's traditional source of livelihood and wealth – the riverside and its commerce. Already placed in a most advantageous position at the western edge of Europe, Lisbon transformed into a highly efficient port could once again become the main Atlantic entrepôt, the crossroad of trade both westward towards the Americas and southwards to Africa and the Far East.

The first step in this restoration would be the complete refurbishment of the maritime buildings of the dockland; they would also be connected to adjacent warehouses and outlets by an efficient system of electrically driven trams or underground trains. Not only would this transport system link the needs of maritime trade to commerce and even to the nearby agricultural producing areas but it would also provide efficient passenger transport, ferrying users from one location to another in minutes. Telegraphic and telephonic services would be available in all of these locations, ensuring immediate and 24-hour communication. Invoices and stocks would be recorded by the latest technology; every possible convenience would be at the disposal of foreigners with the object of making Lisbon the most attractive port in Europe.

Melo de Matos's vision was startling in its modernity but it was also a revamping of the traditional role of the maritime Lisbon. His central railway station, the 'Lisboa Mar', would be the nerve-centre linking all those trading activities described three centuries earlier by Damião de Góis as the lifeblood of Lisbon. But now it would take a mere two minutes to travel from the docks to the commercial area of the Baixa, the heart of the old Manueline city. Even there Melo de Matos saw the need to modernize buildings so that they would function more efficiently in the new order. The neoclassical façades of Pombalese buildings would be maintained but their interiors would be entirely gutted to meet the needs of utility. New buildings would be fenestrated in an unelaborated manner, blending in with the straight lines of the existing ones. The commercial centre of the city would also be linked to the industrial complexes that were growing up on the south bank of the Tagus by a tunnel, entirely up to date and serviced by a high-speed train. Melo de Matos's engineering background is evident in his setting out of the precise measurements of the tunnel, which would be 6327 metres long and 22 metres below the river.

Melo de Matos's modern vision was fuelled by a grand ambition of the sort that had inspired King Manuel at the beginning of the sixteenth century. His purpose, like the king's, was to transform a backward-looking city into a state-of-the-art metropolis which would continue to function, but very much more effectively, as the centre of empire as well as of worldwide commerce. Melo de Matos's statement was an extraordinarily optimistic one in the last years of the monarchy; in the context of the First Republic, established in 1910, it soon began to look just as unattainable. For despite some important reforms – the separation of Church and State, the guarantee of the right to strike, some public support for the destitute and the modernization of social law (allowing divorce for the first time), and symbolic gestures that included a new flag[1] – the Republic remained torn apart by ideological divisions which prevented the economic growth necessary to support such a bold civic gesture in the capital.

The provisional government of the First Republic was presided over by the distinguished figure of Teofilo Braga, writer and intellectual of the old republican school. Braga was by this time nearing 70 years of age and, like many other radicals of student days,[2] he now cut a respectable figure in the eyes of conservatives at home and abroad. But being welcomed by the heads of states of mostly monarchical European countries did not necessarily stand him in good stead among the more radical, socialist elements among the republicans. The split between the two wings of the movement hardened, particularly as the left was associated with more extreme hardline socialism. Although the setting up of the republic met the aspirations of the political middle classes, it did not eliminate extreme political action, including a continued campaign of bombing by the anarchists. The labour movement itself had become infiltrated by radical elements bent on destroying the state. In 1911 there was a general strike: that event and other graphic images of Lisbon during this period were captured in the evocative photographs of Joshua Benolliel.[3]

In the immediate aftermath of the revolution that ended the monarchy, only republicans ran for election, although in some cases the official republican candidates were challenged by more radical left-wingers. A central body tried to keep a tight control on who was adopted. Gradually, groups on the political right began to emerge. The inherently liberal constitutional set-up was undermined by economic instability; as conditions continued to deteriorate, civil unrest increased. That in turn led to demands for stricter government.

In 1917 the uneasy experiment with parliamentary democracy came to an abrupt end: Sidónio Pais was installed as dictator with sweeping powers after a coup in Lisbon while several key figures in the government were abroad. Pais was himself a military man who presided over a highly divided administration. The north of the country was virtually ungovernable. The new regime had no greater success with the economy than its predecessors; a spiralling balance-of-payments deficit and conscription for military service in the Allied cause in Flanders increased tension among the middle classes. The government was convinced that supporting the Allied cause was the only way of preserving the colonial empire. Among the lower classes, particularly in Lisbon, life was grim. Starvation was not unknown. For many people their only option was to emigrate and the numbers leaving Portugal for Brazil increased significantly. Splits in the republican movement became more apparent in the ensuing elections and a monarchist party made its first appearance.

Only a year later, in 1918, Sidónio Pais was assassinated in Rossio station, surrounded by ministers, generals and other dignitaries. Three years later, António Granjo, the prime minister, and a leading group of politicians were also assassinated. Political murders and arson attacks scarred the face of Lisbon. By 1926, after 45 changes of government with no prospect of stability, the forces of the right (including monarchist elements) were once again ready to back a military ruler. General Gomes da Costa, commander-in-chief of the army, took over but, despite his stern disciplinarian approach, lacked the administrative or financial skills to fulfil the role of head of state convincingly. A further period of turbulence and upheaval seemed to be beginning.[4]

Despite the political turmoil of the years of the First Republic, the fabric of Lisbon continued to change and a modern city began to emerge, if not in the futuristic way envisaged by Melo de Matos. The spread, as before, was in a northerly direction away from the river. The two main squares, the Praça Maquês de Pombal (also known as the Rotunda) at the far end of the Avenida da Liberdade and the Praça Saldanha to the north-east, were linked by the Avenida Fontes Pereira de Melo, running alongside the Parque Eduardo VII, named in honour of the English king's visit in 1903. The apartments flanking the park, in the Portuguese 'suave' style, became highly fashionable residences for the upper bourgeoisie. Beyond Saldanha grew up what seemed to be an entirely new city with the aptly named Avenida da República stretching in a north-westerly direction towards Campo Grande, for the first time directly linked to the other main squares. The plan for this arterial expansion of squares and avenues was developed over several decades. Improvement in transport, particularly with the introduction of electric trams, made commuting from areas outside the commercial centre much easier. Something of Melo de Matos's vision inspired Ressano Garcia, the leading planner of the expanding city; public funds became easier to acquire under the *Estado Novo* or new Salazarist regime, which was intent on promoting patriotism by the building of grand national monuments. As the avenues spread across the city, apartment blocks appeared as residential accommodation for the middle classes and the aspiring petite bourgeoisie, providing comfortable sanctuary in what was otherwise an increasingly intense urban environment. The poorer areas tended to be towards the east; they were characterized by more piecemeal development as they had been in the nineteenth century. Shoddy building and inferior materials showed in the fabric of these buildings and gave the areas a slum-like appearance.

Nevertheless there was sufficient architectural activity to raise a new consciousness about the outside features of buildings and their interiors. The Society of Portuguese Architects was founded in 1902, much influenced by French taste, which began to show itself on the façades of the new avenues. Art nouveau features became popular; they were sometimes embellished with a Manueline flourish. Before the shortages of the First World War, decorative features included elaborate ironwork overportals and entrances or as additions to balconies and window frames. Buildings designed for industrial use were sometimes constructed of metal, with pointed pillars supporting the roof so that space within the structure was maximized. The art nouveau style also made its appearance, particularly in decorative rather than architectonic features. The wavy lines of art nouveau finished off entrances along the new boulevards, which were themselves reminiscent of Paris whence the style had come.

At certain points along the broad avenues, for example on Avenida Almirante Reis, the connection with the old Moorish city was kept alive by the construction of ornamental water heads or fountains, particularly on corners and at intersections.[5] That connection was confirmed by the use of multicoloured *azulejo* patterns of plants and flowers that were prominent features of the new style. Meanwhile art deco also became popular on the façades of buildings in the Baixa or in popular rendezvous like the Cervejaria Moderna. One of the most florid examples of the style is to be found at the Animatografo do Rossio, a cinema built in 1907.[6] Its three entrances are encased in elaborate wooden mouldings depicting twisted plants in a high Manueline manner. In the other direction, on the slope of the Rua do Carmo, was the department store Grandella, built in 1904. Its elaborate façade dominated the street for over eighty years until it was destroyed in a fire in 1988. Sixa Veira, the architect commissioned to rebuild it, was careful to restore its eclectic mix of the nouveau and deco styles.[7]

The mixture of these two styles during the modernist period was reflected in fenestration across the city. Many of the *azulejo* tiles

used were manufactured in the Fabrica de Faianças in Caldas da
Rainha. The manufacturer deliberately incorporated traditional,
Manueline features into the motifs, so that a distinctive Portuguese
mix was achieved. The same inspiration can be found in the tiles
produced by the Fabrica de Louça at Sacavém or in Lisbon itself
at the Fábrica Lusitana between 1910 and 1930. The geometric
designs of the architect Raul Lino emphasized the more modernist
aspects of these design changes.[8]

Meanwhile what might be described as a traditional-modernist
regime was being established in the political world. In 1926 a
military movement, soon to be known as the National Revolution,
emerged; middle-class opinion began to harden against democratic
arrangements which seemed unable to stem the tide of anarchy.
As a series of generals struggled to grapple with the worsening
financial crisis, it became apparent that only a leader with sweeping
powers and a financial grip was going to succeed in getting control
of the situation. In 1928 President Carmona invited Antonio de
Oliveira Salazar, a professor of economics at Coimbra University,
to join the government. His mandate was to restore economic
order, an essential prerequisite of political stability. However,
the professor turned out to have more radical plans. He was not
concerned with merely establishing financial good health but was
determined to introduce a new political order. Within four years
he took complete control of government.

Salazar planned his seizure of absolute power in a series of carefully prepared moves. His ideological programme was based on a
new constitution in 1933 setting up the *Estado Novo* or New State,
which was approved in a plebiscite. The new constitution drew to
some extent on the nineteenth-century Charter.[9] It emphasized
the power of the executive as against parliament. Salazar was
deeply anti-communist, portraying the communists as unpatriotic
subversives bent on destroying the national identity of Portugal.
Instead he offered a paternalistic regime, focused on preserving
the empire and the Portuguese mission associated with it. His

personal austerity lent credibility to his role as a Sebastianistic protector of the nation-state. In the new order, authority was concentrated in the hands of the president, who was elected by universal suffrage, thus bypassing the parliamentary mechanism. Although parliamentary elections took place, the nomination of candidates was in the hands of a body, the National Union, controlled by the state rather than by political parties. The head of government was the prime minister; he was the effective power in the land and had complete control of the legislature, which never opposed him.

Within this rigid structure, Salazar ruled the country for forty years, keeping a tight personal grip on all aspects of policy, whether domestic or foreign. The authoritarian nature of the regime was protected by a ban on the formation of political parties throughout the period; a rigorous censorship of the media ensured that opposition to the government's policy was extremely muted. At the centre of the corporate state was the political police, the PVDE (Policia de Vigilancia de Defesa do Estado), whose methods of operation were a modernized version of the Inquisition.[10]

However, the principal reason why Salazar's rigid control of political life was tolerated was because of his success in the economic sphere. His policy was based on a tight fiscal control with wages kept low and barely any inflation. Although the latter factor kept the prices of staples low, it also resulted in a low standard of living for the working class, among whom there was a level of illiteracy as high as 40 per cent. The main beneficiary of his policies was the middle class, whose standard of living was protected. It was in their economic interests, therefore, to support the regime even if they had doubts about its oppressive character. Moreover, by austere management of public funds so that the books were balanced year by year, sufficient surpluses were created for many public projects, modernizing the infrastructure of the country. Like the fascist regimes in Germany and Italy, Salazar concentrated on road building and the relocation of public offices from the monastic premises that had been seized from the Church to new, dedicated buildings that themselves advertised the power of the New State. A bridge was built over the Tagus (and two over the Douro); under the direction of Duarte Pacheco, a system of radial periphery roads enabled traffic to move around Lisbon with much greater ease. Lisbon's harbour was modernized; an airport was built; dams and reservoirs were constructed. This revamping of Lisbon's infrastructure greatly enhanced middle-class life; the political stability that allowed it appeared in stark contrast to the chaos and disorder of the First Republic. Opposition to the regime and frustration at the lack of means of democratic expression remained muted among the more politically articulate section of society. As Fernando Pessoa (1885-1935), later to be recognized as Portugal's greatest modern poet, wrote in 1932:

> I don't want to get drawn into discussions of the New Constitution and the Corporate State; I accept them both as disciplines. I keep myself clear of them because I don't agree with them.[11]

Despite the considerable signs of urban regeneration on the fringes and littoral of the city, the core of old Lisbon did not greatly change. It was in this old quarter that Fernando Pessoa passed his secluded but febrile days. Pessoa was born in Lisbon but had spent his childhood in South Africa (his stepfather was the Portuguese consul at Durban). He was fluent in English as a result of his education there. However, when once he had returned to Lisbon to attend university, he hardly travelled again, confining himself largely to the old centre areas of the Baixa and the Bairro Alto. He expressed a fear of even crossing the Tagus, lest on his arrival at the other side there should be nothing. His joy at his return to Lisbon is celebrated in his poem 'Lisbon Revisited'. The poet declares:

> I see you once more,
> City of my childhood now frighteningly lost
> City mournful and gay, once more in you I dream[12]

Dreaming or daydreaming was central to Pessoa's intellectual thought and to his poetry, which is cerebral as well as intensely lyrical despite its modernist trappings. He claimed indebtedness to Césario Verde, poet of Lisbon, who in the nineteenth century had written his verse in a mood of sensory realism.[13] Pessoa's notion of the city was abstract, even hallucinatory, but it forms an indispensable backcloth to the poetry. His existence on the sloping streets of the Bairro Alto, marching down the Rua do Alecrim to Caís do Sodré or in the grid-like Baixa, was intensely localized.[14] Travel became a metaphysical experience for Pessoa. Since a sunset in the Chiado was as good as a sunset in China (and considerably more accessible), there was no need to set foot outside the confines of old Lisbon. Nevertheless the particular environment of the old quarter, with its elaborate façaded buildings, sloping alleyways and dead ends with views of the sea, greatly influence the mood of his universalist musings, abstract though they are. The features of the city made up the elements of the world in which his spirit wandered; they are elliptically echoed throughout his verse. Indeed, in his existentialist way, Pessoa claims that as a living creature with a soul he is only marginally different from the buildings and warehouses among which he lives.

Nor did Pessoa inhabit these quarters alone; he created a host of other personalities in his 'heteronyms' or different voices in which he chose to write. The three most prominent Pessoan characters are Ricardo Reis, Alvaro do Campos and Albert Caeiro. Each wrote in a different style, ranging from the neoclassical to the romantic and the popular. A fourth voice was that of Bernardo Soares (author of Pessoa's *Book of Disquietude*), whose character was closest to his creator's but who lacked the ironic and self-deprecating edge that Pessoa showed when writing about himself. For Soares, as for Pessoa himself, the Baixa is a village; the bells of the Igreja dos Martires in the Chiado are the local sound which establishes the particularity of the place. Striding around these old, closed-in streets whether to take his *bica* (espresso coffee) or something stronger at the Café Brasileira in the Rua Garrett or the Martinho in the Praça do Comércio, Pessoa is almost always alone, smoking his way through three or four packets of cigarettes a day. Occasionally he meets someone at one of the modest restaurants he frequents for dinner. Were any of these Masonic encounters? Sometimes one of the heteronyms is his dinner companion. Bernardo Soares dines in the same kind of restaurants as his creator, before retiring to his lodgings where he spends his evenings writing. The Pessoan universe can focus on a single street – such as the Rua dos Douradores in the Baixa where Pessoa happens to be living.

Pessoa, like Alberto Pimentel,[15] delighted in Lisbon mornings. He walks the deserted streets in the light mist that comes up from the sea before dawn. The shutters of the houses are still closed and the clatter of the daily life does not begin until the marketers arrive to put up their stands. This is the time for the artist and writer to soak up the spirit of the city, the layers of meaning and unmeaning that are folded in its dust, accumulated over the ages. Pessoa talks of inhaling the mist into his very being; it helps his creation of an evanescent and abstract locale for his poetry. Soon the cheerful, mindless chatter of the *saloios* (the peasants) on their way to work will interrupt the tranquillity (which may be disturbing as well as restful). But up to that point the only distraction is the smell and the sound of the sea, something that Pessoa understood to be the essence of Lisbon's existence. In the *Maritime Ode* the poet senses the mystery of the sea and the act of embarkation from the shore.

> Who knows? Who knows if I never
> Embarked before, myself from such a quay?
> As a ship in the oblique rays of the morning sun, who knows
> If I have not sailed from a different kind of port?[16]

Pessoa's love of maritime Lisbon is part of his deeply felt patriotism. In his travel guide to Lisbon,[17] he dwells upon the majestic seafaring associations of the Tower of Belém, a monument of fragile beauty which, once enveloped by the waves, was now joined to the land itself. Pessoa of course knows his history. He may admire the filigree finesse of the Manueline style of Belém's castellation but he also knows about the dark side of the tower as a place of incarceration and human suffering. The city's secrets are part of the sometimes sad and grim story of its political history.

The Lisbon that Pessoa quitted, on his death in 1935, was entering another bold phase of architectural evolution in the hands of the generation known as the 'first modernists'. The most prominent of these was Cassiano Branco (1898–1969), the architect. A graduate of the Escola de Belas Artes, his most impressive achievement was an art deco building, the Eden cinema, at the beginning of the Avenida da Liberdade near Rossio. He also designed a purer example of the modernist style at the Hotel Vitória, further up the avenue. Cassiano Branco was a man of the left with strong political opinions. Like Pessoa, he had an uncomfortable relationship with the Salazar regime. His grand, ambitious designs can be understood as a protest against the more restrained and utilitarian public works supported by the government. As a result much of Cassiano's work was done in the private sector, avoiding the need for official approval and public funding. His design in the area of domestic architecture included the first example, in the Rua Nova de São Mamede, of continuous fenestration, a row of windows curving around the side of a building, uninterrupted by any partitioning or divides.

Nevertheless the Eden cinema remained his grandest and most utopian design, the idea of which was to create a palace of escapism along the most modern and stylish lines. This quest for the ideal is reflected in the neoclassical façade of the building, which has perpendicular pillars, headed by a horizontal frieze of art deco figures in marble. The effect is to give the building a temple-like appearance. The symmetry and strength of his design rely on emphasizing structural lines. In this way, the art deco embellishments are given a solid foundation. Cassiano Branco built other

cinemas – the Império along another avenue – and he understood
their symbolic value in a strictly regulated society. Nevertheless he
must have realized that even in these retreats it was not possible to
escape the long arm of the Salazarist state, since films continued
to be heavily censored.

Modernism also had its adherents in the plastic arts. By 1939,
a group of artists, including Maria Helena Vieira da Silva, had
established themselves as an independent cadre within the Sociedade Nacional de Belas Artes. These artists were regarded with
considerable suspicion even though their style was largely abstract
and, in the case of Vieira da Silva, worked in the traditional metier
of *azulejos*. Nevertheless, recognizing that they were a force to
be reckoned with, the government decided to coax them into the
service of the *Estado Novo*. Vieira da Silva chose to leave the
country rather than succumb to official blandishments; others
remained in Portugal struggling on as best they could without
compromising their art.

The year 1940 represented the high point in the achievement of
the *Estado Novo*. To commemorate 800 years of nationhood, as
well as the three-hundredth anniversary of the restoration of Portuguese independence after the 'Spanish domination' (1580–1640),
the regime organized a great exhibition, together with a series
of events and publications on historical subjects. The Exhibition
of the Historic Portuguese World was meticulously prepared; the
best contemporary architects and artists were commissioned to
contribute to what was to be a highly patriotic event. The exhibition was inaugurated at the historically important area of Belém,
with its rich associations with the explorations. A large site of 45
hectares was cleared on the banks of the Tagus near the Tower of
Belém. Displays included ethnographical and historical representations of Portugal and the colonies; there was a highly slanted
ideological theme to the whole exhibition. As befitted the capital
of empire, Lisbon had a dedicated pavilion, as did Brazil, the most
glittering of the Portuguese colonies. Maritime and industrial

themes complemented imperial ones; Portugal was represented as the centre of a united lusophone world. The exhibition ran for six months. Its main symbol, the caravel, was echoed in a dramatic construction erected to the east of the Tower of Belém by Cottinelli Telmo in the next generation.[18] Telmo's massive sculpture, in the shape of the prow of a caravel, is a monument to the explorers. A procession of figures is headed by Prince Henry the Navigator, in his familiar broad-brimmed hat, himself cradling a ship in his hands. He is followed by Dom Manuel, Camões, the explorer Diogo Cão and a procession of seafaring folk, shipbuilders, soldiers and priests, all veritable servants of the nation.

Salazar's Portugal maintained neutrality during the Second World War but was broadly sympathetic to the Allied cause. As the only continental point of contact between the two sides, Lisbon became the centre of espionage and counter-intelligence activities of both the Allies and the Nazi regime in Berlin. It was also a place of relative comfort in a war-torn Europe, suffering only the occasional blackout. The British MI6 agent and writer Graham Greene was responsible for Portuguese operations 1943–44. Several colleagues from this period found their way as characters into his fictional work. One of the more dramatic coups during his time was an exchange of intelligence with the French Resistance smuggled into Lisbon in the form of musical scripts. Life for Portuguese inhabitants of Lisbon was less protected. The political police (PVDE) continued to persecute ruthlessly those whom it regarded as enemies of the state. Recruiting their members from the brain-washed Youth Movement (Mocidade Portuguesa), PVDE extended its activities into monitoring all kinds of behaviour that might be regarded as decadent or anti-social, even discouraging any display of affection in public. The traditional Lisbonite response was in subtle references to political matters in popular music (*fado*), in wall cartoons and satirical theatre. Individuals practising any of these forms of criticism became expert at knowing exactly how to tread a thin line without incriminating themselves. These two aspects of Lisbon life – the espionage and the political repression – are captured in many novels of the pre-war and wartime city, most brilliantly in António Tabucchi's novel about a journalist, *Declares Pereira*.[19]

It was to this labyrinthine Lisbon that Rose Macaulay came in 1943. She was already a distinguished writer of the pre-war Bloomsbury period. Suffering personal loss in the London Blitz (including a library of books) she arrived in neutral Portugal where there was considerable sympathy with the beleaguered Britain. She settled into a modest hotel in the Avenida da Liberdade, beginning her research at the British Institute and in the archives of the British Historical Society of Lisbon on the English men and women who had come to Portugal. From the start she loved the old cobbled streets and hilly alleyways of the city. Her second visit took place in 1947, when some of the restrictions of the wartime city had been lifted. Like Southey before her she delighted in the Alfama, with its twisted narrow streets, and she imbibed the Baroque excesses of the old churches of Lisbon. On this second visit she was also able to explore the coast as far as Cascais, and of course to pay the obligatory pilgrimage to Beckford and Byron's Sintra. Her contribution to the story of the English in Lisbon is itself part of the history of the foreigners' city.

The immediate post-war period was to prove a difficult one for the country as a whole. Lisbon, which lost its cachet as an international centre of espionage, now looked once again like a provincial city struggling to keep control of its vast tracts of colonial territory in Africa. One Portuguese historian ascribes the depressed atmosphere of this period to the activities of the secret police (now known as PIDE),[20] whose activities became ever more intrusive of the private life of citizens. Various state decrees had put their activities beyond the ordinary processes of law. Contact with the German SS who had been stationed in Lisbon during the war may have encouraged members of PIDE to regard themselves as the engine of the New State and the guardians of public morality.

Their methods, which included the use of torture, had all the hallmarks of extreme intimidation associated with fascist regimes. Nevertheless, even in these difficult circumstances, there was a mobilization of the left. The Communist Party, though banned, played an important part in the organization of strikes, aimed at paralysing the public services. Unrest in the universities was also articulated in political pamphleteering, sometimes done in the samzidat style that had been a feature of intellectual protest in Russian and Soviet society.

It was of course easier for writers and intellectuals of the right to operate without interference. The South African poet Roy Campbell, who was violently anti-socialist, went to live in Portugal in 1952. He produced translations of Eça de Quierós and Pessoa, as well as of Spanish literature, in which he was more of an expert. His prose work on Portugal was published in 1956. In the introduction to the book, Campbell compares Salazar to Afonso Henriques, thus conferring upon him the highest accolade as a patriot.[21] Another foreigner who came to Lisbon at this time who would contribute significantly to the cultural life of the city was the Armenian entrepreneur Calouste Gulbenkian. When he died in 1955 he left a vast fortune and an important, eclectic collection of paintings and *objets d'art* to the city of Lisbon. This collection was to be housed in the specially built Gulbenkian Museum off the Praça de Espanha in the old Palhavã park, once used by the bastard sons of King João V. A foundation, dedicated to the promotion of Portuguese culture, was also established and became one of the most prominent patrons of the arts in the country. Despite the sometimes gloomy atmosphere of these years, Lisbon continued to be a subject of inspiration for artists who stayed there. Carlos Botelho's scenes of sloping roofs and ordinary houses, surrounded by scenes of daily activity against a backdrop of the river, bring the city to life. He is especially good at capturing the fading light that has led to the comparison of the Tagus estuary with a sea of straw.[22] Artists less sympathetic to the regime, like Paula Rego, chose to leave the country and paint abroad, sometimes confronting the regime with critical portraits of life in contemporary Portugal.

At a communal level, the cafés, centres of liberal dissent during the monarchy,[23] once again became the fora where opposition to the regime was to be found.[24] Given the degree of infiltration by PIDE and its ruthless methods of inquisition, habitués of the Lisbon houses were careful what they said about politics in public. Salazar himself expressed little concern at the activities of a tiny minority of literary-minded intellectuals. A new generation of writers, including Fernando Namora, Urbano Tavares Rodrigues and David Mourão-Ferreira, followed Pessoa's footsteps to the Café Brasileira in the Chiado. Being the only places of animation in the city (and acting for some as an escape from dreary homes) the cafés attracted students, who went to do their work in them, and artists, who discussed their work with others. The Nicola, now established in new premises, in Rossio, sported a fine art deco façade; the Suiça, on the other side of the square, was famous for its hot chocolate.

Equally places of escape, the cinemas (São Jorge, Imperial, Alvalade, Monumental, Tivoli and São Luís) built in the previous decades enjoyed huge popularity. The bourgeoisie turned up at the cinema in its finery; intervals in the middle of the show provided opportunities for an informal fashion parade to take place. Although the censor's scissors were still at work (sometimes rendering the plots of films unintelligible), the cinema offered an escape from the sometimes grim reality of city living, as it has done to generations of younger Parisians in another congested city centre. Sometimes the cinemas were used to stage carnival celebrations of a theatrical type, in which masked figures and fancy dress were de rigueur. Carnival itself, the traditional pagan celebration of spring, was one of the few occasions when control of public events was relaxed. Other non-political activities, whether that of horse dressage connected with bullfighting or increasingly popular football, were encouraged by the regime as ways of keeping the masses entertained and distracted from political activities.[25]

As on so many other occasions in its long history, the next challenge that came to Portugal and to its capital originated overseas. The regime was obsessively committed to the myth of empire. Salazar himself, an ascetic and reclusive figure, was steeped in messianic *Sebastianismo*, seeing himself as the guardian of Portuguese nationalism, which had started with the expulsion of the Moors and was consolidated with the achievement of the explorations. His devout Catholicism added another traditional element to an ideology presented in new wrappings but which was in essence similar to that of his royal precursors. Lisbon, regenerated by new building programmes and kept spruce, remained a showpiece for stability and order. In 1966 the Ponte Salazar (later renamed the Ponte 25 Abril), one of the longest suspension bridges in Europe, was opened, connecting the city to the growing urban sprawl of Almada on the south side of the river. The scale of this enterprise symbolized the continuing ideological vision of the city as centre of empire. Nevertheless, before long, the very structure of the *Estado Novo* came under attack: in particular, Portuguese colonial policy began to look increasingly out of date in the 'winds of change' continent of Africa of the early 1960s. In the sixteenth century Portugal's territorial ambitions had been checked in Morocco; in the twentieth century her overseas role was challenged and brought to an end the colonies of Guinea, Angola and Mozambique further south and south-east on the same continent.

As Portugal came under increasing criticism from the international community, the argument that its overseas territories were part of the metropolitan country (confirmed by the so-called organic law of 1953) was less and less convincing. The guerrilla warfare in the African colonies meant that a whole generation of Portuguese young men would spend their early years fighting a war which the military became convinced could not be won. Public confidence was further undermined in 1961 when the Indian army drove the Portuguese out of Goa. However insignificant a conclave Goa had become, the forced retreat was symbolically important. At the same time the war in Africa began to drain the surpluses that Salazar had carefully built up during years of tight fiscal management. Public-sector investment had to be slowed down. The middle classes that had most benefited from the Second Republic saw their savings begin to be eroded at the same time as their sons, conscripted to serve in the war, were killed in distant lands. Casualties mounted into tens of thousands. Even so, opposition was slow in developing. In 1961 Henrique Galvão, in a spectacular coup, seized the liner *Santa Maria* but the government stood firm and refused to negotiate. In 1965 Humberto Delgado, the opposition, leader was assassinated, most likely by the PIDE.

When Salazar fell ill in 1968[26] Marcelo Caetano took over the reins of power. Another professor (this time of administrative law), he seemed more liberal than Salazar. Events in France that year suggested the need to loosen the reins of rigid censorship that made books like the *New Portuguese Letters*,[27] challenging orthodoxy in a number of ways, still proscribed. Nor did Caetano take any steps to dismantle the political institutions of the *Estado Novo*. Moreover, he also showed that he had no intention of changing the policy in Africa. The colonial wars continued but by now were beginning to become unpopular among the military itself. The officers in charge of the colonial campaigns shared the view that there was no military solution to the wars; at the same time the government showed no willingness to seek a political solution. This impasse led a group of serving officers to the conclusion that there would be no change to the situation unless the regime was overthrown: the Armed Forces Movement (MFA) was born. At dawn on 25 April 1974 a column of soldiers advanced on central Lisbon, seizing important buildings including the PIDE headquarters. There was no resistance and within hours the be-monocled figure of General António Spinola became the unlikely head of a revolutionary regime. Political prisoners were freed, hard-core PIDE members were rounded up, and within days new democratic elections were promised. The revolution had been almost bloodless; the citizens of Lisbon lined the streets to scatter red carnations (the symbol of the revolution) on the troops. Within a year the African empire (consisting of the Cape Verde Islands, São Tomé e Príncipe, Guinea, Angola and Mozambique) was disbanded.

The immediate consequence for Lisbon was an enormous inflow of immigrants, reckoned to number 700,000. The airport became a vast refugee camp, and in and around Lisbon sprang up shanty-towns all too familiar to those who had served in Africa. The economic and cultural impact of the *retornados* (those who have returned) was considerable. Among them were some who were capable of organizing themselves into communities of mutual support; others brought an invigorating entrepreneurial flair to their adopted country. Like other European cities with colonial pasts, Lisbon was accelerated into a new cosmopolitanism, although the different races were not always integrated. Immigrant ghettoes, such as the black one in Monsanto, sprang up in different parts of the metropolitan area.

In the post-1974 period the city expanded its boundaries considerably. Some of the suburban sprawl, lacking proper infra-structure, became a dangerous breeding ground for drug-taking and violence. Erstwhile semi-rural areas to the west of the city disappeared in a suburban spread; the coastal 'villages' along the Estoril line were engulfed by the appearance of large and densely populated apartment blocks. After the entry of Portugal into the European Community in 1986, a generously funded programme led to extensive new road building around Lisbon. A system of ring roads grew up, while the old city centre (particularly around the Chiado) began a long process of regeneration which continues to the present day. Buildings untouched for generations began to be refurbished for modern, middle-class living; city life traditionally hidden behind closed doors, or in cellars, spilt out into the street, symbol of a new and unfamiliar lack of inhibition. On the littoral below the old city, warehouses were redeveloped to accommodate a new generation of Lisbonites who were intensely proud of being members of the European Community.

To the east of the city, a massive redevelopment programme was put in place, culminating in the area known as the Parque das Nações, where the Expo exhibition of 1998 was held. The central feature of this redevelopment, echoing the spirit of Melo de Matos, is the Gare do Oriente, a massive glass and steel rail terminal. This futuristic building, with its vast open interior space, also picks up traditional themes, some of which, such as the palm trees with glass leaves, resurrect Manueline exuberance. The monumental terminus is connected to the new metro system, now extending over central Lisbon. Water features in the shopping arcades once again echo the theme of the sea.

In the Utopian Pavilion (renamed the Atlantic Pavilion) the most patriotic symbol of Portugal, the caravel, is used again in a dramatic and original form of an upturned hull. Nearby the Pavilhão de Portugal picks up the maritime theme by its fantastical wave-like series of concrete shapes which sweep across an open plaza, strung over by a concrete canopy, the work of Alvaro Siza Vieira. The concrete sheet created in this way is suspended from the top of the walls of the building. On an island within the complex is the Oceanarium, one of the largest in the world, while concrete towers, the modern equivalents of medieval structures, are placed at different points in the site. During Expo itself each part of the Luso-colonial world, including the far-flung provinces of Macao and East Timor, was represented in small pavilions and stands. Stretching across the river from near the site is the Vasco da Gama Bridge, the first major crossing of the Tagus near the city since the Salazar Bridge of the 1960s. The seven-mile road that it forms weaves across the river in an undulating form, spectacularly lit at night.[28]

The rebuilding of such a vast area of Lisbon might suggest an entirely new phase in its development, modern and forward-looking. Yet despite the modernistic appearance of the buildings, many of their decorative features hark back to traditional, patriotic symbols. The very site of the new area, on the littoral facing the wide river, reflects the old city's links with the sea. Nearby there is a bridge, symbolically linking it to the beyond, the 'other side'. The stalls of empire were to be found in Expo transformed into stalls of a lusophone world that bears little relation to the European Community that Portugal has now joined. Saramago has suggested that even as a member of the European Community, Portugal has remained marginal (as it was as a far-flung province of the Roman Empire) and he symbolizes this by showing the whole Peninsula drifting off as an island into the Atlantic Ocean towards the Azores.[29] Nor has the assimilation of immigrants from the old colonies always been easy. Problems to do with the accommodation of the African *retornados* have still not been settled 30 years later; Brazilians (sharing the Portuguese language) complain of being treated as second-class citizens despite the country's addiction to Brazilian soap operas. Although the younger generation of Lisbon-ites show signs of a more expansive 'European' and even American spirit and enjoy the new commercial opportunities brought about by global contact, there remains something inward-looking, lan-guid and illusive in the air of the old city.

In 1983 Alain Tanner produced the film *The White City,* which graphically presented this dreamlike, hallucinatory character of Lisbon. In the film, this impression is emphasized when the old Pombalese city, seen from a headland on the river bank, appears to arise out of the mist. Leaving the seashore, if we walk up to one of the many elevated parks or *miradouras* at São Pedro de Alcãntara at the edge of the Bairro Alto, we can still look across towards the castle and gain another impression of the city lying below us in a valley, once bucolic. Turning our gaze to the right, we come back again to the river, the source of inspiration for generations of Lisbonites, as Sophia de Mello Breyner so poignantly reminds us.

Here and there as we walk Lisbon's streets
In a hurry or lost in thought
Turning the corner we suddenly see
The shimmering blue of the Tagus
And our body becomes light
Our soul is winged.[30]

Chronological Table

1m BC	*Homo erectus* comes to the Iberian Peninsula from Africa, until 200,000 BC
20,000 BC	Paleolithic remains: Coa Valley, Escoural, Alentejo
5500 BC	Neolithic remains along Tagus estuary
1000 BC	Phoenicians reach southern Portugal, founding Olisipo
700 BC	Celtic tribes invade northern Portugal
600 BC	Greek traders in Portugal
535 BC	Carthaginian occupation of Portugal
218 BC	Roman invasion of the Iberian Peninsula
219 BC	Resistanceof Lusitani
139 BC	Death of Viriatus
	Romanization of Lisbon area
	Roman theatres, temples and baths in city
25 AD	Roman province of Lusitania
410	Alaric the Visigoth sacks Rome
	Suevi in Portugal
	Visigoths in Spain
475	Extinction of Western Roman Empire
585	Visigothic Kingdom of Hispania
711	Moorish invasion of Iberian Peninsula
	Moorish castle (Alcoçava) built
833	Reconquest of northern Portugal by Christians
950	Portucale established

1139	Battle of Ourique
1147	Siege and capture of Lisbon by Afonso Henriques
1160	Sé Cathedral founded
1179	Charter of Lisbon; Portugal recognized by Pope
1255	Lisbon becomes capital of Portugal
1290	University founded in Lisbon
1333–34	Famine caused by crop failure
1348	Plague kills 40 per cent of population
1355	Death of Iñes de Castro
1372	Siege of Lisbon by D. Henrique II of Castile
1385	Battle of Aljubarrota
1386	Treaty of Windsor
1415	Capture of Ceuta
1419	Madeira discovered
1487	Bartolomeu Días rounds the Cape of Good Hope
1494	Treaty of Tordesillas
1497–98	Vasco da Gama discovers the sea route to India
1500	Pedro Alvares Cabral discovers Brazil
1502	Jerónimos Monastery started
1505	D. Francisco de Almeida becomes Viceroy of India
1506	Race riots and pogrom in Lisbon
1516	Garcia de Resende's *Cancioneiro Geral*
1521	Tower of Belém completed
1526	São Roque Church started
1529	Gil Vicente's *Triunfo do Inverno*
1536	Office of the Inquisition established
1544	Bernardim Ribeiro's *Menina e Moça*
1554	Damião de Góis's *Urbis Olisiponis descriptio*
1572	Luís Vaz de Camões's *Lusiads*
1578	King Sebastião's war council at Sintra and defeat at Alcácer-Quibir in Morocco
1580–1640	United kingdom of Spain and Portugal
1703	Methuen Treaty
1740s	Rose café opened
1755	Lisbon earthquake; Pombal becomes prime minister
1787	William Beckford's first visit to Lisbon
1790s	Café Nicola opened
1796	Robert Southey's first visit to Lisbon
1807	French invasion; royal family leave for Brazil
1809	Byron's visit to Sintra
1810	Battle of Buçaco; Wellington's Torres Vedras lines
1812	Byron's *Childe Harold*
1822	Liberal constitution

1825	Almeida Garrett's poem *Camões*
1828-34	Civil war in Portugal
1832	Office of Inquisition abolished
1834	Expulsion of religious orders; closing of monasteries
1840	Pena Palace at Sintra started
1851	Beginning of period of Regenerators, Historicals and Progressives
1874	Lamanjat rail link from Lisbon to Sintra
1886	Avenida da Liberdade opened
1888	Eça de Queirós's *Maias*
1890	British ultimatum on Africa
1901	Santa Justa elevator in operation
1906	Melo de Matos's *Lisboa no anno 2000*
1908	Assassination of King Carlos and crown prince
1910	Revolution; First Republic established
1917	Sidónio Pais becomes president
1926	*Coup d'état* of General Gomes da Costa
1928	Salazar becomes minister of finance
1930s	Modernist movement in the arts (Cinema Eden)
1933	*Estado Novo*
1949	Portugal enters NATO
1960	Cottinelli Telmo's monument at Belém
1965	Assassination of Humberto Delgado
1966	Suspension bridge across the Tagus
1968	Salazar succeeded by Caetano
1974	Revolution of 25 April
1976	Second Republic established
1986	Portugal joins European Union
1998	Expo held in Lisbon

Kings, Queens and Rulers of Portugal

Afonsin dynasty

1128-85	Afonso Henriques *m.* Mafalda of Maurienne and Savoy
1185-1211	Sancho I *m.* Dulce of Aragon
1211-23	Afonso II *m.* Urraca of Aragon
1223-48	Sancho II *m.* Mécia Lópes de Haro
1248-79	Afonso III *m.* (1) Matilde, Countess of Boulogne (2) Beatriz de Guillén
1279-1325	Dinis (the Husbandman) *m.* Isabel of Aragon
1325-57	Afonso IV *m.* Beatriz of Castile

1357–67   Pedro I (the Cruel) *m.* (1) Bianca of Castile (2) Constanza of
           Castile (3) Ines de Castro
1367–83   Fernando I *m.* Leonor Teles
1383–85   Interregnum

Avis dynasty

1385–1433 João I *m.* Philippa of Lancaster
1433–38   Duarte I *m.* Leonor of Aragon
1438–81   Afonso V (the African) *m.* Isabel of Portugal
1481–95   João II *m.* Leonor of Portugal
1495–1521 Manuel I (the Fortunate) *m.* (1) Isabel of Castile (2) Maria of
           Castile (3) Leonor of Spain
1521–57   João III *m.* Catarina of Spain
1557–78   Sebastião (the Regretted)
1578–80   Henrique (the Cardinal-King)
1580   António, Prior of Crato

Austrian dynasty (Spanish kings)

1580–98   Filipe I (Filipe II of Spain)
1598–1621 Filipe II (Filipe III of Spain)
1621–40   Filipe III (Filipe IV of Spain)

Bragança dynasty

1640–56   João IV *m.* Louisa de Gusmão
1656–83   Afonso V *m.* Maria-Francisca-Isabel d'Aumule of Savoy
1683–06   Pedro II (regent from 1668) *m.* (1) Isabel d'Aumale (2) Maria-
           Sofia-Isabel of Neuberg
1706–50   João V (the Munificent) *m.* Maria-Ana of Austria
1750–77   José *m.* Mariana-Victoria of Spain
1777–1816 Maria I *m.* Pedro de Bragança
1816–26   João VI (regent from 1792) *m.* Carlota-Joaquina of Spain
1826–28   Pedro IV (abdicated) *m.* (1) Maria Leopoldina of Austria (2)
           Maria-Amelia of Leuchtenberg
1828–34   Miguel *m.* Adelaide-Sofia of Loewenstein-Rosenberg
1834–53   Maria II (da Gloria) *m.* (1) August of Leuchtenberg (2)
           Ferdinand of Saxe-Coburg-Gotha
1853–61   Pedro V *m.* Stéphanie of Hohenzollern Sigmaringen
1861–89   Luís *m.* Maria-Pia of Savoy
1889–1908 Carlos *m.* Marie-Amélie of Orléans
1908–10   Manuel II (the Unfortunate) *m.* Augusta-Victoria of
           Sigmaringen

Bragança dynasty in Brazil

1822-31	Emperor Pedro I
1831-89	Emperor Pedro II

Presidents or heads of provisional governments

1910	Teófilo Braga
1911-15	Manuel de Arriaga
1915	Teófilo Braga
1916	Bernardino Machado
1917-18	Sidónio Pais
1918-19	Admiral João de Canto e Castro
1919-23	António José de Almeida
1923-25	Manuel Teixeira Gomes
1925-26	Bernardino Machado
1926	Commander Mendes Cabeçadas
1926	General Gomes da Costa
1926-51	General António Carmona [António de Oliveira Salazar prime minister 1932-68]
1951-58	General Francisco Lopes
1958-74	Admiral Américo Tomás [Marcelo Caetano prime minister 1968-74]
1974	General António Sebastião Ribeiro de Spinola
1974-76	General Francisco da Costa Gomes
1976-86	General António dos Santos Ramalho Eanes
1986-96	Mário Alberto Nobre Lopes Soares
1996	Jorge Sampaio
2006	Cavaco da Silva

Notes

Acknowledgements

1. C.A. Montalto, *Historic Macao* (Hong Kong, 1902; 2nd enlarged edn Macao, 1926; republished Oxford, 1984).
2. See *The Lisbon Earthquake of 1755: Representations and Reactions* (ed. T.E.D. Braun and J.B. Radnor) (Oxford, 2005).

Chapter 1

1. The origin of the city's name is also difficult to pin down. The Phoenician name was Alis Ubo; while the Roman city was called Olisipo; recent opinion suggests that Lixbona (meaning 'good water') was the Latin source for Lissabona and Lisboa of modern Portuguese. The Germanic name for the city was Ulixbuna, the Moorish Al-Usbana. See A. Crespo *Lisboa Mítica e Literária* (Lisbon, 1990) pp. 46 ff.
2. See Malcolm Jack, *Sintra: A Glorious Eden* (Manchester, 2002) p. 20.
3. The Cabo da Roca was known as the 'Rock of Lisbon' to seafarers.
4. L.V. de Camões, *The Lusiads* (trans. L. White) (Oxford, 1997) pp. 59, 93. The term 'Luso' is usually associated with the heroic figure Lusus (associated with the god Bacchus) but it has also been linked to the biblical city of Luz. See Crespo, *Lisboa Mítica e Literária*, p. 46.

5. See G. Pereira de Castro, *Ulisseia ou Lisboa Edificada* (ed. J.A. Segurado e Campos) (Lisbon, 2000).

6. The Phoenician name for Lisbon, 'Alis ubbo', translates as 'pleasant inlet'. J. Laidlar, *Lisbon*, World Biographical Series, vol. 199 (Oxford, 1997) pp. xxiii, xxiv.

7. Roy Campbell remarked about living in a time 'when tradition and myth are being asserted and confirmed more and more by archaeological investigation'. *Portugal* (London, 1957) p. 24.

8. The skulls of human beings, recently found in Ethiopia, suggest that *Homo sapiens* originated in Africa in that period.

9. Cave drawings of a similar type (depicting hybrid creatures partly human, partly animal) have emerged in different parts of the world, including Southern Africa, dating from the same period.

10. The origin of the name Tagus may be from the Phoenician word *Dagvi*, meaning 'plentiful fish'.

11. Laidlar, *Lisbon*, p. xxiv.

12. See I. Moita, 'Das origems pré-históricas ao domínio Romano', in *Livro de Lisboa*, ed. I. Moita (Lisbon, 1994) pp. 25-34.

13. A. H. de Oliveira Marques, *História de Portugal*, 3 vols (Lisbon, 1984) vol. 1, p. 16.

14. So described by Camões in Canto III of *The Lusiads*, p. 60.

15. See J. Cardim Ribeiro, 'Estudos histórico-epigráficos em torno da figura de I. Julius Caudicus', in *Sintra I-II tomo I 1982-1983* (Mem Martins, 1984-87) pp. 151-477.

16. Other municipalities in Lusitania included Mertola (Myrtilis), Evora (Liberalitis Julia) and Alcácer do Sal (Salacia). They were fortified towns (*oppidi*), each governed by a commission of two magistrates.

17. Excavations at the Cathedral took place in 1990. See J.L. de Matos, 'As excavaçoes no interior do Claustro da Sé', in *Livro de Lisboa* (ed. I. Moita) (Lisbon, 1994) pp. 32-4.

18. De Oliveira Marques, *História de Portugal*, vol. 1, p. 48.

19. The concept of reconquest stems from the claim of continuity with the Visigothic kingdoms of the Iberian Peninsula in place prior to the Moorish invasion. See de Oliveira Marques, *História de Portugal*, vol. 1, pp. 128 ff.

20. See A. Borges Coelho, *Portugal na Espanha Arabe*, 2 vols (Lisbon, 1989) vol. 1, p. 236.

21. See Illustrations.

22. J. Saramago, *The History of the Siege of Lisbon* (trans. G. Pontiero) (London, 1996) p. 133.

23. Ibid., p. 155.

24. J. Read, *The Moors in Spain and Portugal* (London 1974) p. 159.

25. D. Couto, *História de Lisboa* (trans. C V da Silva) (Lisbon, 2003) p. 50.

26. Ibid., p. 54.

27. See C.R. Boxe, *The Portuguese Seaborne Empire* (Manchester, 1991) p. 10.

28. H.V. Livermore, *Portugal* (Edinburgh, 1973) p. 56.

29. Couto, *História de Lisboa*, pp. 69-70.

30. From J. Munzer 'Ulixbona, known as Lisbon Today' in *Lisbon before the 1755 Earthquake: Panoramic View of the City. An Anthology of Texts on Lisbon from XV to XVII Centuries* (ed. P. Henriques, trans. M. de Brito) (Lisbon, 2004) pp. 39-40.

31. This is noted by the French historian Bourdon, who ascribes it to cultural development of Portuguese identity based on language. A.A. Bourdon, *Histoire du Portugal* (Paris, 1994) p. 7.

32. Livermore, *Portugal*, p. 63.

33. Nuno Álvares Pereira (1360-1431) came from an aristocratic background. He epitomized the image of the valiant knight, the ultimate patriot dedicated to national service and public well-being. Pereira's daughter married a bastard son of João I, founding the eventually royal Bragança dynasty.

34. Quoted in Livermore, *Portugal*, p. 67.

35. Madeira is classified by some Portuguese historians as a 'rediscovery' as it was probably visited in the fourteenth century and certainly in 1419. See Couto, *História de Lisboa*, p. 118.

36. For a classical account of Prince Henry's role see E. Bradford, *Southward the Caravels* (London, 1961). This heroic stature of Prince Henry has been challenged by British and Portuguese historians. See P. Russell, *Prince Henry 'The Navigator'* (Yale, 2000) *passim*, and Couto, *História de Lisboa*, p. 117.

37. Nun'Álvares himself had mysteriously retired to a monastery. See de Oliveira Marques, *História de Portugal*, vol. 1, p. 228.

38. Munzen, 'Ulixbona', pp. 47-8.

39. Livermore, *Portugal*, p. 77.

Chapter 2

1. Bradford, *Southward*, p. 163.

2. An account of his voyage was published in 1540 by a priest named Francisco Alvares. It was read with interest by Samuel Johnson when he was preparing *Rasselas, Prince of Abysinnia*, itself published in the year of the Lisbon earthquake of 1755.

3. De Oliveira Marques, *História de Portugal*, p. 16. The early explorers left *padrões* or stone markers along the coasts they discovered.

4. Bourdon, *Histoire du Portugal*, p. 54.

5. Portuguese claim to the sovereignty of Macao was to become a major issue once the British were ensconced in nearby Hong Kong. See C. Montalto, *Historic Macao, passim*.

6. For a full account of Magellan's voyage, see L. Bergreen, *Magellan's Terrifying Circumnavigation of the Globe* (London, 2003).

7. See Illustrations.

8. See Illustrations.

9. For the fullest account of what is known about the building in Dom Manuel's time, see A. Delaforce, *Art and Patronage in Eighteenth-Century Portugal* (Cambridge, 2002) pp. 3 ff.

10. The tapestries themselves were collectively known as the 'Conquest of India'. The detailed instructions about their subject matter were given by António Carneiro, chief royal secretary. See ibid., p. 7.

11. See J.A. França, *Lisboa Urbanismo e Arquitectura* (Lisbon, 1997) p. 15.

12. Garcia de Resende (1470-1536), a native of Evora and polymath figure who was musician, singer, historian, designer as well as poet.

13. Inês de Castro was a Spanish courtier murdered by courtiers (who distrusted her connections with Spain) while King Pedro I (1320-1367) was away from the court. When the king returned, he had her body exhumed and forced the courtiers to pay homage to her corpse in a grotesque and bizarre ceremony. Despite his sobriquet the 'Cruel', accounts suggest the king was a popular, generous figure.

14. Gil Vicente (1465-1537), something of a biographical mystery, was a leading Portuguese dramatist.

15. Francisco de Sá de Miranda (1487-1558) studied law in Lisbon and was well-read in classical literature and in contemporary European writings.

16. Bernardim Ribeiro (*c.* 1480s-*c.* 1530s). Little is known about his life or the production of his works some of which were anonymous, though he may have studied at Lisbon University between 1507 and 1511.

17. Francisco de Holanda (1516-1584). Born in Lisbon, perhaps with little formal education he was interested in classical antiquities, architecture, history and art; as well as being a talented classicist, linguist and painter.

18. From 'The Islands', Sophia de Mello Breyner, *Log Book: Selected Poems* (trans. R. Zenith) (Manchester, 1997) p. 88.

19. See Illustrations.

20. Charles Dellon, 'De l'Inquisition de Goa', in *Lisbon before the 1755 Earthquake*, pp. 86-7.

21. F. Pessoa, *Lisbonne* (Paris, 1995) p. 70. Also see Illustrations.

22. Aquilino Ribeiro (1885-1963) in *Arcas Encoiradas* (1949).

23. See Jack, *Sintra,* pp. 53 ff.

24. See W.C. Watson, *Portuguese Architecture* (London, 1908) pp. 117, 136 ff.

25. For a full discussion of the Manueline style, see M.C. Mendes Atanazio, *A arte do Manuelino* (Lisbon, 1984).

26. Jack, *Sintra*, pp. 59 ff.

27. De Oliveira Marques, *História de Portugal*, vol. 2, p. 75.

28. Damião de Góis, born in Alenquer in 1502, died in Lisbon in 1574.

29. The book is dedicated to Prince Henry the Navigator. The only other European city worthy of the description might be Seville on account of its role in the Spanish American trade. D. de Góis, *Lisbon in the Renaissance* (trans. J. Ruth) (New York, 1996) p. 3.

30. Góis records Asclepiades Mirlianus' claim that physical remains, including shields, garlands and spurs belonging to Ulysses were found in Lisbon. Ibid., p. 8.

31. Ibid., p. 20.

32. Ibid., p. 24.

33. Ibid., p. 28.

34. The account ends with a paean to the town of Alenquer, along the Tagus estuary, birthplace of the author.

35. See J.-A., França, *Lisboa: Urbanismo e Arquitectura* (Lisbon, 1997) pp. 16-18.

36. Dellon, 'De l'Inquisition de Goa', p. 96.

37. F. le Tours, 'Voyage d'Espagne et du Portugal', in *Lisbon before the Earthquake of 1755*, p. 105.

38. This work took the form of two elegant dialogues, in the style of Plato's *Republic*, setting his view of the city in a political and economic context. See Luís Mendes de Vasconcelos, *Sitio de Lisboa*, 1608.

39. Tirso de Molina (*c.* 1584-*c.* 1645) dramatist, writer of religious works and of fiction.

40. For example by D. Vieira Serrão of 1650. Also see Illustrations.

Chapter 3

1. Known also as the great Mother of the Gods, her cult was celebrated in spring; see J. Warrington, *Everyman's Classical Dictionary* (London, 1961) p. 351.

2. See Jack, *Sintra*, p. 30.

3. Moita, *Livro de Lisboa*, p. 40.

4. See above p. 13.

5. See Jack, *Sintra*, p. 53 ff.

6. See Illustrations. We need to bear in mind that subsequent changes, for example in twentieth-century restoration, have altered the original appearance.

7. André de Resende wrote a poem on the subject of St Vincent, published in 1545.

8. See Illustrations.

9. See Illustrations.

10. See above, p. 45.

11. Frei António das Chagas (1631-1682) was one of the most significant figures of the Baroque period. Educated at the Jesuit college at Evora, he wrote widely on religious and spiritual subjects.

12. *Arquivo Histórico de Sintra*, 34 vols (ed. J.M. da Silva Marques) V, p. 9-10.

13. The atmosphere of terror is well captured in R. Zimler's novel, *The Last Kabbalist of Lisbon* (London, 1998).

14. J. Saramago, *The Gospel According to Jesus Christ* (trans. G. Pontiero) (London, 1997) p. 298. See Illustrations on Sintra Inquisition.

15. Floyd's activities are described by Rose Macaulay, *They Went to Portugal Too* (Manchester, 1990) pp. 98 ff.

16. His career or lack of it is discussed in M. Ataide, 'A Igreja da Santa Graça', in *Livro de Lisboa* (Lisbon, 1994) p. 284.

17. For a comparison of his work and that of Portuguese Baroque church architects, see S. Sitwell, *Portugal and Madeira* (London, 1955) pp. 23 ff.

18. He also supported the performing arts and it was in this period that Doménico Scarlatti (1685-1757) resided in Lisbon, composing both sacred and secular music at court.

19. Johann Friedrich Ludwig (1673 -1752). He came to Portugal in 1701, having been trained in Rome, to work for the Jesuits.

20. William Beckford later gave a Gothic description of the court at Queluz. See Malcolm Jack, *William Beckford: An English Fidalgo* (New York, 1996) p. 72.

21. Mateus Vicente de Oliveira (1710-1785); Jean Baptiste Robillon (d. 1782).

22. The impressive façade of the parliament building was added in 1876.

Chapter 4

1. Part of the high ground of this area had subsided after the earthquake of 1531.

2. F. de Tours, 'Voyages d'Espagne et Portugal', in *Lisbon before the Earthquake of 1755*, p. 108.

3. See above, pp. 74-5.
4. For a detailed account of the treasures of the royal palace, see A. Delaforce, *Art and Patronage*, pp. 1-116.
5. Ibid., p. 71.
6. Anon., 'An account by an eye-witness of the Lisbon earthquake of 1 November 1755', *British Historical Society of Portugal* (Lisbon, 1985) pp. 5-6.
7. Ibid., p. 6.
8. Ibid.
9. Ibid.
10. Couto, *História de Lisboa*, p. 185.
11. K. Maxwell, *Pombal, Paradox of the Enlightenment* (Cambridge, 1955) p. 24.
12. Ibid.
13. T.D. Kendrick, *The Lisbon Earthquake* (London, 1955) p. 32.
14. *Commentario Latino e Portuguez sobre o terramoto e incendio de Lisboa* (Lisbon, 1756).
15. Kendrick, *The Lisbon Earthquake*, p. 32.
16. See Illustrations for ruins of St Nicholas.
17. D. Francis, *Portugal, 1715-1808* (London, 1984) p. 123.
18. *Select Letters of Voltaire* (ed. T. Besterman) (London, 1963) p. 150.
19. Kendrick, *The Lisbon Earthquake*, p. 122.
20. Gabriel Malagrida (1689-1761) was an Italian who had become a celebrated missionary in Brazil. His pulpit eloquence was matched by alleged miraculous powers. He had been well received by King João V in 1749, whose confessor he became and at whose deathbed he was present. He was friendly with the aristocratic Tavora family.
21. Kendrick, *The Lisbon Earthquake*, p. 89.
22. Ibid.
23. See ibid., pp. 159-61.
24. Voltaire, *Romans et Contes* (ed. H. Bénac) (Paris, 1960) p. 116 (author's translation).
25. See J.-J. Rousseau, 'Lettre à M. Voltaire', *Œuvres Complètes* (Paris, 1971) 3 vols; vol. 2, pp. 316-42.
26. Fernando Pessoa, *Selected Poems* (trans. P. Rickard) (Edinburgh, 1971) p. 163. For an informative essay on the influence of the earthquake and its imagery in Portuguese literature, see E.J. Vieira, 'Coping and Creating after Catastrophe: The Significance of the Lisbon Earthquake of 1755 on the Literary Culture of Portugal', in *The Lisbon Earthquake of 1755* (ed. T.E.D. Braun and J.B. Radnor) (Oxford, 2005) pp. 282-97.
27. J.J. Moreira de Mendonça, *Historia Universal dos Terramotos* (Lisbon, 1758).

28. Sebastião José de Carvalho e Melo, Marquês de Pombal (1699–1782) was born into the ranks of the lower aristocracy. After a period managing the family's country estates in the north of Portugal, he began a diplomatic career that saw him posted first to London and then to Vienna from 1739 to 1750. His political career took a decisive turn when he was appointed a minister by King José in 1750. His experiences abroad and a certain distrust of the British interest in Portugal helped to shape his policies when he was in office. See Illustrations.

29. A Portuguese biographer has described him as being 'perspicacious' rather than 'original'. See A. Bessa Luis, *Sebastião José* (Lisbon, 1984) p. 53.

30. Francis, *Portugal*, p. 122.

31. De Oliveira Marques, *História de Portugal*, vol. 2, p. 353.

32. See Illustrations.

33. Maxwell, *Pombal*, p. 26.

34. Pina Manique (1733–1805) was sympathetic to the plight of the ordinary Lisbon people, whom he, like Pombal, believed should be properly protected by an absolutist but benign authority. One of his lasting reforms was the setting up of the charitable institution the Casa Pia for looking after orphans. A great political survivor, he managed to remain in office after Pombal's fall in 1777.

35. The notion of Lisbon rising like a phoenix from the ashes as Rome had done from the ashes of Troy was a powerful symbol. See Vieira, 'Coping and Creating after Catastrophe', p. 290.

36. Maxwell, *Pombal*, pp. 46–7.

37. For a detailed account of his efforts, see Francis, *Portugal*, p. 89.

38. Goudar blamed much of the Portuguese weakness on superstition and the influence of the Church, another sentiment that Pombal would have shared with him. See A. Goudar, *Relation historique du Tremblement de Terre...* (à la Haye, 1756).

39. Quoted in Delaforce, *Art and Patronage*, p. 289.

40. Maxwell, *Pombal*, p. 25

41. See Delaforce, *Art and Patronage*, p. 295.

Chapter 5

1. See above, pp. 11ff.

2. For Osbern's account, see *De Expugnatione Lyxboniensi* (ed. C.W. David) (New York, 1936).

3. In 1373 Lisbon had been sacked by Enrique II of Castile, showing how real the threat was.

4. See above, pp. 29ff.

5. See *An Account of the Court of Portugal under Pedro II* (London, 1700).
6. R. Twiss, *Travels in Spain and Portugal in 1772 and 1773* (London, 1775); J. Murphy *Travels in Portugal* (London, 1795).
7. See Malcolm Jack, 'The World of Beckford's Portuguese Palaces' in *William Beckford, 1760–1844: An Eye for the Magnificent* (ed. D. Ostergard), Catalogue of an Exhibition at the Bard Graduate Center for Decorative Arts, New York (New Haven and London, 2001) p.89.
8. Beckford's particular friend was Diogo José Vito de Menezes, 5th Marquis (1739-1803), Grand Master of the Horse, Gentleman of the Bedchamber, General and Councillor of War.
9. Murphy, *Travels in Portugal*, p. 197.
10. For an account of the summer of 1787, see Jack, *William Beckford*, pp. 27-52.
11. W. Beckford, *The Journal of William Beckford in Spain and Portugal 1778-88* (ed. Boyd Alexander) (London, 1954) p. 58.
12. João Carlos de Bragança (1719-1806), 2nd Duke, 'Uncle of the Queen' and grandson of Pedro II. Later married Henriqueta de Marialva (daughter of the 5th Marquis). His palace, Grilo, was east of Lisbon.
13. Beckford, *The Journal*, p. 110.
14. See Jack, *William Beckford*, p. 110.
15. See J. de Almeida Flor, 'Portuguese Tears and Treasures: On Beckford's Literary Fortune' *The Annual Lectures of the Beckford Society 1996-1999* (Wiltshire, 2000) p. 30.
16. George Gordon, Lord Byron, *Childe Harold's Pilgrimage*, Canto I, Stanza XVI, in *Poetical Works* (Oxford, 1967) p.183.
17. Ibid., pp. 183-4.
18. For a full account of the Convention and British reactions to it, see M. Glover, *Britannia Sickens: The Convention of Cintra* (London, 1970).
19. See R. Macaulay, *They Went to Portugal* (London, 1946) pp. 173ff.
20. Byron, *Childe Harold*, p. 874.
21. See M. Newitt and M. Robson, *Lord Beresford and British Intervention in Portugal 1807-1820* (Lisbon, 2004).
22. J. Baretti, *Journey from London to Genoa* (intro. I. Robertson) (London, 1970) p. 95.
23. Ibid., p. 112.
24. See Illustrations.
25. Ibid., p. 189.
26. M. Link, *Voyage en Portugal depuis 1797 jusqu'en 1799* (Paris, 1803).

27. Hans Christian Andersen, *A Visit to Portugal, 1866* (trans. G. Thornton) (London, 1972) p. 19.
28. António Feliciano de Castilho (1800-1875), educated at Coimbra, publishing his first poem on the death of Queen Maria I at the age of 16. Also see Illustrations.

Chapter 6

1. For a full account of the royal years in Rio, see K. Schultz, *Tropical Versailles* (New York and London, 2001). The difficult crossing to Rio is described in P. Wilcken, *Empire Adrift* (London, 2005).
2. Ferdinand Augustus Antonius Kohary de Saxe-Coburg Gotha (1816-1885) was son of the Duke of Saxe-Coburg Gotha. He assumed the title of king in 1837 after the birth of an heir. See Illustrations.
3. The letter is part of an important collection of private papers. See M. Ehrhardt, 'Dom Fernando artavés das suas cartas à familia', in *Romantismo – Figuras e factos da epoca de D. Fernando II* (Sintra, 1988).
4. Dom Fernando was a talented engraver. Some of his work can be seen at the Ducal Place at Vila Viçosa, the Bragança country seat and later summer residence of the royal family.
5. See below, pp. 138 ff.
6. Dom Luís, his son, took to translating Shakespeare into Portuguese, whilst Dom Carlos, his grandson, was a watercolourist. A collection of Dom Carlos's paintings can also be seen at the Ducal Palace of the Braganças at Vila Viçosa.
7. See above, p. 191 n34.
8. Tinop drew much of his source material from contemporary newspapers, bulletins and institutional archives, both official (e.g. Aviso e cartas do Reino) and academic (e.g. Memórias da Académia Real das Ciências), as well as from histories and literature. Pinto de Carvalho, *Lisboa D'Outros Tempos* [1898] 2 vols (Lisbon, 1991).
9. Ibid., vol. 1, p. 18.
10. Ibid., vol. 2, p. 20. Tinop's second volume is given over to the subject of Lisbon's cafés.
11. Couto suggests that the café was founded in 1782. *História de Lisboa*, p. 208.
12. Whether it was the popular Lisbon tipple of cherry brandy is not clear.
13. Named after its Italian owner, Nicola das Parras.
14. Filinto Elísio (1734-1819). This was the pseudonym of Father Manuel do Nascimento, a skilled Latinist and musician who translated French literature as well as producing his own verse.

15. Manuel Maria l'Hedoux de Barbosa du Bocage (1765-1805), who, although hailing from a cultivated, middle-class family, was not conventionally educated, joining the army in his teens.
16. Nicolau de Tolentino Almeida (1740-1811) had a very different life from Bocage. From the earliest days, he deferred to aristocratic patrons, thereby gaining preferment in various prestigious, academic institutions in the reformed education system introduced by Pombal. Nevertheless, he remained capable of turning his wit on himself as a practitioner of the 'unhappy art of satire'.
17. The street and area took its name from António Ribeiro Chiado (c. 1520-1591), poet, dramatist and writer of religious works.
18. For the classic account of this group on intellectuals abroad, see V. Nemésio, *Exilados 1828-1832* (Lisbon, c. 1976).
19. See below, p. 142.
20. It is fitting that the elegant street Rua Garrett, named after him, is in the heart of the Chiado, linking the Rua do Carmo to the Largo do Chiado. Some, like the poetess Fernanda de Castro (1900-1994), have preferred to keep to the simpler name of Chiado for the street. On the other side of the slope is the Praça L. de Camões, where the poet is commemorated with a statue.
21. See Illustrations.
22. The most notable literary salon was that of the Marquesa de Alorna. Also on Castilho, see above p. 123.
23. Of the Necessidades and Ajuda both to the west of the city centre. Fialho de Almeida, writing at the beginning of the twentieth century, makes a plea for the educational role of the Ajuda library, with its well-stocked humanist collection. Fialho de Almeida, *Lisboa Monumental* (Lisbon, 1906) pp. 55-6.
24. The five artists were Tomás Anunciação, Francisco Metrass, José Rodrigues, Vitor Bastos and Cristino da Silva himself.
25. The Spanish critic Angel Crespo has said that to know Lisbon one has to be away from her.
26. A. Pimentel, *Fotografias de Lisboa* [1874] (Lisbon, 2005) p. 15.
27. Published posthumously in 1903.
28. Fialho de Almeida (1857-1911).
29. Couto, *História de Lisboa*, p. 230.
30. See Illustrations.
31. R. Campbell, *Portugal,* p. 193.
32. See above, pp. 63 ff.
33. Jack, *Sintra*, pp. 192-3.
34. The park just north of the Rotunda (Pombal) was named in celebration of the visit. A close confidant of the English king at home was the Marquis of Soveral, ambassador to the Court of St James's

and a considerable figure in Edwardian society.

35. A moving account of the last days of the monarchy is given in the queen's diary. See S. Bern, *Eu, Amélia, Ultima Rainha de Portugal* (trans. D.C. Garcia) (Barcelos, 1999).

Chapter 7

1. And a new unit of currency, the escudo, which survived until the introduction of the euro in 2001.

2. Joaquim Teofílo Braga (1843-1924) was part of the Coimbra school of writers, which included Antero de Quental in the 1860s and which challenged literary establishment thinking. He was the author of a number of influential books on history and religion. Also see above, p. 153.

3. Joshua Benolliel (1873-1932) worked for a long period for the influential journal *Ilustração Portuguesa*. The events of the strike and period of unrest are also recorded by Raul Brandão (1867-1932) in his *Memórias* (Lisbon, 1911).

4. Oliveira Marques records the occurrence of 36 coups, revolts and assassinations between 1911 and 1926. See Oliveira Marques, *História de Portugal*, vol. 3, p. 287.

5. See Illustrations.

6. The cinema now shows pornographic films. Its façade appeared in João Cesar Monteiro's bizarrely evocative film about the sleazier side of Lisbon, *Recordações da Casa Amarela* (1989).

7. The department store was first opened in 1885 by Francisco Grandella, one of the first industrialists to understand the important link between production and consumer demand.

8. Despite these professional leanings, Lino was also interested in medieval architecture and wrote a book about the old palaces of Sintra. See Jack, *Sintra*, p. 54.

9. See above, pp. 126, 139. There was also a link between the ideology of the *Estado Novo* and the notion of the *República Nova* of Sidónio Pais. See J. Hermano de Saraiva, *Portugal: A Concise History* (Manchester, 1997) p. 112.

10. See Saramago's definition above, p. 71.

11. Quoted in de Saraiva, *Portugal*, pp. 112-13.

12. *Fernando Pessoa: Selected Poems* (ed. and trans. P. Rickard) (Edinburgh, 1975) p. 91.

13. José Joaquim Césario Verde (1855-1886) whose reputation among the modernists of the twentieth century was very high.

14. The area around the station was the old seamakers' quarters; the station itself was the sea carpenters' centre.

15. Pimentel talks of walking the streets of Lisbon early in the morning to gain the best impression of the city. Pimentel, *Fotografias*, p. 17.
16. Translated by Roy Campbell, *Selected Poems* (ed. M. Chapman) (Johannesburg and Cape Town, 2004) p. 141.
17. Written in English, probably in 1925, under the title *Lisbon: What the Tourist Should See*, it was eventually published posthumously in 1992.
18. See Illustrations.
19. Published in English in 1995, Robert Wilson's spy romance *In the Company of Strangers* (2001) and most recently Domingos Amaral's novel *Enquanto Salazar dormia* (2006) continue to re-create the spy-ridden atmosphere of the wartime city.
20. See Couto, *História de Lisboa*, p. 295. PIDE was the acronym for Policia Internacional e de Defesa do Estado.
21. R. Campbell *Portugal* (London, 1957) p. viii.
22. 'Mar de Palha'.
23. See above, pp. 135 ff.
24. As always the influence of France on Portuguese intellectuals was considerable during this period when left-wing intellectuals dominated French political life.
25. Benfica football club was founded in 1904.
26. He died in 1970.
27. Published in 1968 by the 'Three Marias'.
28. Modern images of the city, including the redevelopment of the docks, are captured in the striking images of Maluda.
29. J. Saramago, *A Jangada de Pedra* (Lisbon, 1986).
30. Sophia de Mello Breyner, *Log Book*, p. 108.

Bibliography

Archives

Arquivo Histórico, Arquivo Municipal, Sintra.
British Library, London.
Museu da Cidade (City Museum), Lisbon.
Torre do Tombo (National Archives), Lisbon.

Secondary Sources

Afonso. S.L., and Delaforce, A. *A Palácio de Queluz: Jardins.* Lisbon,
 1989.
Alexander, B. 'Beckford's Debt to Portugal'. *The British Historical Society
 of Portugal.* 5th Annual Report and Review. Lisbon, 1978.
Amaral, D. *Lisboa enquanto Salazar dormia.* Lisbon, 2006.
Amarante, E. *Portugal Simbólico, Origens sagradas dos Lusitanos.* Lisbon
 1999.
Andersen, H.C. *A Visit to Portugal* 1866 (trans. G. Thornton). London,
 1972.
Anderson, B., and E. *Landscapes of Portugal. Sintra. Cascais. Estoril.*
 London, 1995.
Andrade. E. de, and Alves, A. *Daqui Houve Nome Portugal.* Oporto,
 1968.

Anon. 'Letter from an Eye-witness of the Lisbon Earthquake'. *British Historical Society of Portugal*. Lisbon, 1985.

Atanazio, M.C. Mendes. *A arte do Manuelino*. Lisbon, 1984.

Atkinson, W.C. *A History of Spain and Portugal*. London, 1960.

Barretti, J. *A Journal from London to Genoa* (intro. I. Robertson). London, 1970.

Barros, C.V. da Silva. *Four Altars to the Virgin*. Lisbon, 1978.

Beckford, W. *Recollections of an Excursion to the Monasteries of Alcobaça and Batalha* (ed. B. Alexander). Fontwell, 1992.

———. *Sketches of Spain and Portugal in the Travel Diaries of William Beckford of Fonthill* (ed. G. Chapman). Cambridge, 1928.

———. *The Journal of William Beckford in Spain and Portugal 1787–88* (ed. B. Alexander). London, 1954.

Bergreen, L. *Magellan's Terrifying Circumnavigation of the Globe*. London, 2003.

Bern, S. *Eu, Amélia, Última Rainha de Portugal* (trans. D.C. Garcia). Barcelos, 1999.

Bombelles, Marquis de. *Journal d'un Ambassadeur de France au Portugal 1786–1788* (ed R. Kann). Paris, 1979.

Borges Coelho, A. *Portugal na Espanha Arabe*, 2 vols. Lisbon, 1989.

Bottineau, Y. *Portugal*. Norwich, 1957.

Bourdon, A.A. *Histoire du Portugal*. Paris, 1994.

Boxer, C.R. *The Portuguese Seaborne Empire*. Manchester, 1991.

Bradford, E. *Southward the Caravels*. London, 1961.

Bradford, W. *Sketches of the Country, Character and Costume in Portugal and Spain*. London, 1809.

Breyner, S. de Mello, *Log Book: Selected Poems*. Manchester, 1997.

Bridges, A. and Lowndes, S. *A Selective Traveller in Portugal*. London, 1949.

Brito, M.C. de. 'A Música no tempo de William Beckford', in *William Beckford: An Impassioned Journey*, Catalogue Raisonné of an exhibition at the Palace of Queluz, Portugal. Lisbon, 1987.

Buck, P. *Lisbon*. Oxford, 2002.

Byron, George Gordon, Lord. *Poetical Works*. Oxford, 1967.

Cabral, A. *Southey e Portugal 1774–1800*. Lisbon, 1959.

Campos, Correia de. *Monumentos de Antiguidade em Portugal*. Lisbon, 1970.

———. *Portugal*, London, 1957.

Campbell, R. *Selected Poems*. Johannesburg and Cape Town, 2004.

Camões, Luís Vaz de. *Lusiads* (trans. L.V. White). Oxford, 1997.

Candeias, A. *Portugal em Alguns Escritores Ingleses*. Lisbon, 1946.

Carneiro, J.M.M., et al. *Palácio Nacional da Pena*. Lisbon, 1987.

Carvalho, G. *Itinerários Temáticos de Lisboa*. Lisbon, 2003.

Carvalho, M. de. *A God Strolling in the Cool of the Evening.* London, 1997.

Carvalho, Pinto de (Tinop). *Lisboa d'Outros Tempos* [1898]. Lisbon, 1991.

Castro, G. de, *Ulisseia ou Lisboa Edificada* [1636] (ed. J.A. Segurado e Campos). Lisbon, 2000.

Centano, Y.K. (ed.). *Portugal: Mítos Revistados.* Lisbon, 1993.

Chorão, J.B. *Nossa Lisboa dos Outros.* Lisbon, 1999.

Colbatch, J. *An Account of the Court of Portugal under Pedro II.* London, 1700.

Corprechot, L. *Memories of Queen Amélie of Portugal.* London, 1915.

Costa, F. *Beckford em Sintra no verão de 1787.* Sintra, 1972.

———. *História da Quinta e Palácio de Monserrate.* Sintra, 1985.

———. *O Paço Real de Sintra.* Sintra, 1980.

Couto, D. *História de Lisboa* (trans. C. Veira da Silva). Lisbon, 2003.

Delaforce, A. *Art and Patronage in Eighteenth-Century Portugal.* Cambridge, 2002.

Delumeau, J. *Une histoire du paradis.* Paris, 1992.

Dias, M.T. *A Lisboa de Fernando Pessoa.* Lisbon, 1998.

———. *Histórias de Lisboa.* Lisbon, 2002.

Dicionário das Alcunhas Alfacinhas (intro. F. Santana). Lisbon, 2001.

Domingues, G. *História Luso-Arabe.* Lisbon, 1945.

Ehrhardt, M. 'D. Fernando II visto atravès das suas cartas à família', in *Romantismo Figuras e factos da época de D. Fernando II.* Sintra, 1988.

Estudos Orientais II: O legado Cultural de Judeus e Mouros. Lisbon, 1991.

Etnografia de Região Saloia. Sintra, 1999.

Everyman's Classical Dictionary (J. Warrington). London, 1961.

Fernandes, J.M. *Lisboa em Obras.* Lisbon, 1997.

Festas de Lisboa. Commisão Consultiva das Festas 1990. Lisbon, 1991.

Fialho de Almeida, J.V. *Lisboa Monumental* [1906]. Lisbon, 2001.

Flor, J. *Sintra na Literatura Romântica Inglesa.* Sintra, 1978.

Fragoso, M.A.P. *O Emblema da Cidade de Lisboa.* Lisbon, 2002.

França, J.A. *Lisboa: Urbanismo e Arquitectura.* Lisbon, 1997.

Francis, D. *Portugal 1715–1808.* London, 1984.

Garrett, Almeida J.B. da Silva. *Travels in My Home Country* (trans. J.M. Parker). London, 1987.

Giraud, I. 'La réverie dans les jardins', in *Romantismo.* Sintra, 1986.

Glover, M. *Britannia Sickens. The Convention of Cintra.* London, 1970.

Guerra, A. *Plínio-o-Velho e a Lusitânia.* Lisbon, 1995.

Hibbert, C. *The Grand Tour.* London, 1987.

Inchbold, A.C. *Lisbon and Cintra* (illus. S. Inchbold). London, 1907.

Jack, M. *Sintra: A Glorious Eden*. Manchester, 2002.

———. 'The World of Beckford's Portuguese Palaces', in *William Beckford, 1760–1844: An Eye for the Magnificent* (ed. D. Ostergard), Catalogue of an Exhibition at the Bard Graduate Center for Decorative Arts, New York, 2001. New Haven and London, 2001.

———. *William Beckford: An English Fidalgo*. New York, 1996.

Jackson, Catherine Charlotte, Lady, *Fair Lusitania*. London, 1874.

Janeiro, M.J. Lisboa, *Histórias e Memórias* Lisbon, 2006.

Jean Pillement and Landscape Painting in Eighteenth-Century Portugal. Catalogue of an exhibition at the Fundação Ricardo do Espirito Santo. Lisbon, 1997.

Kennedy, H. *Os Muçulmanos na Península Ibérica*. Mem Martins, 1999.

Kinsey, W. *Portugal Illustrated in a Series of Letters*. London, 1828.

Laidler, J. *Lisbon*. World Biographical Series, vol. 199. Oxford and Santa Barbara, 1997.

Le Roy Liberge, G. *Trois Mois au Portugal*. Paris, 1910.

Lino, R. *Os Paços Reais da Vila de Sintra*. Lisbon, 1948.

Lisbon before the 1755 Earthquake: Panoramic View of the City. An Anthology of Texts on Lisbon from XV to XVII Centuries (ed. P. Henriques, trans. M. de Brito). Lisbon, 2004.

Lisboa, Guia Urbano. Lisbon, 2002.

Livermore, H.V. *Portugal: A Short History*. Edinburgh, 1973.

———. *Portugal: A Traveller's History*. Woodbridge, 2004.

Loução, P.A. *Os Templários na formação de Portugal*. Lisbon, 1999.

Luís, A.B. *João Sebastião*. Porto, 1981.

Macaulay, Rose. *They Went to Portugal*. London, 1946.

———. *They Went to Portugal Too*. Manchester, 1990.

Machado, Álvaro Manuel. *Dicionário de Literatura Portuguesa*. Lisbon, 1996.

Madureira, N.L. *Lisboa Luxo e Distinção 1750–1830*. Lisbon, 1990.

Marques, A.H. de Oliveira. *História da Maçonaria em Portugal*, 2 vols. Lisbon 1996.

———. *História de Portugal*. 3 vols. Lisbon, 1984.

Marques-Gonçalves, J.L. 'Monumento préhistórico da Praia das Maçãs (Sintra) Notícia Preliminar', in *Sintria I–II. tomo I, 1982–83*. Mem Martins, 1984–87.

Massie, I. *Byron's Travels*. London, 1988.

McCarthy, M. *The Origins of the Gothic Revival*. Newhaven and London, 1987.

Melo de Matos. *Lisboa no anno 2000* [1906]. Lisbon, 1998.

Montalto de Jesus, C.A. *Historic Macao* [1902]. Oxford, 1985.

Moreira, R. 'Novo dados sobre Francisco de Holanda', in *Sintria I–II tomo I, 1982–83*. Mem Martins, 1984–87.

Múrias, M.M. *Chiado: do século XII ao 25 Abril*. Lisbon, 1996.

Murphy, J. *Travels in Portugal*. London, 1795.

Nemésio, V. *Exilados: 1828–1832*. Lisbon, 1946.

O Grande Terramoto de Lisboa: ficar diferente (ed. H.C. Buescu and G. Cordeiro). Lisbon, 2005.

O Neomanuelino ou a Reinvenção da Arquitectura dos Descobrimentos. Instituto Português do Património Arquitectónico. Lisbon, 1994.

Oliveira, C.R. de. *Lisboa em 1551*. Sumário. Lisbon, 1987.

Parro, J. *O Chiado*. Lisbon, 1997.

Pereira, P. (ed.) *História da Arte Portuguesa*, 3 vols. Lisbon, 1999.

Pessoa, F. *The Book of Disquietude* (trans. I. Watson). London, 1991.

———. *Lisbon: What the Tourist Should See* [1925], as *Lisbonne* (trans. B. Vierne) Paris, 1995.

———. *Selected Poems*. (ed. and trans. P. Rickard). Edinburgh, 1971.

———. *Selected Poems* (ed. M. Chapman, trans. Ruy Campbell). Johannesberg and Cape Town, 2004.

Picard, C. *Le Portugal Musulman (XVIIe–XIIe siècle)*. Paris, 2000.

Pimentel, A. *As fotografias de Lisboa* [1874] Lisbon, 2005.

Pires, M.L.B. *William Beckford e Portugal*. Lisbon, 1987.

Portugal from Its Origins through the Roman Era. National Museum of Archaeology and Ethnology. Lisbon, 1989.

Povey, J. *Roy Campbell*, Boston, 1977.

Quadros, A. *Portugal Razão e Mistério*, vol. 1. Lisbon, 1999.

Queirós, J.M. Eça de. *O Mistério da Estrada de Sintra*. Lisbon, 1884.

———. *The Maias* (trans. P.M. Pinheiro and A. Stevens). London 1998.

———. *The Tragedy of the Street of the Flowers* (trans. M.J. Costa). Sawtry, Cambridge, 2000.

Quest-Ritson, C. *The English Garden Abroad*. London, 1992.

Reed, J. *The Moors in Spain and Portugal*. London, 1974.

Ribeiro, J.C., et al. *Sintria I–II, tomo I, 1982–83*. Mem Martins, 1984–87.

Ribeiro, O. *Portugal, o Mediterrâneo e o Atlântico*. Lisbon, 1998.

Russell, P. *Prince Henry 'the Navigator': A Life*. Yale, 2000.

Ruth, J.S. *Lisbon in the Renaissance*. New York, 1996.

Sá, V. da *Lisboa no Liberalismo*. Lisbon, 1992.

Salter, C. *Introducing Portugal*. Bristol, 1956.

Santos, P.B., et al. *Lisboa Setecentista Vista por Estrangeiros*. Lisbon, 1992.

Saramago, J. *A Jangada de Pedra*. Lisbon, 1986.

———. *Baltasar and Blimunda (Memorial do Convento)* (trans. G. Pontiero). London, 1998.

———. *História do Cerco de Lisboa*. Lisbon, 1989.

———. *Viagem a Portugal*. Lisbon, 1981.

Saraiva, A.J. *O Que é a cultura*. Lisbon, 2003.

Saraiva, A.J. and Lopes, O. *História da Literatura Portuguesa*, 17th edn. Oporto, 1996.

Saraiva, J.H. *Portugal: A Companion History*. Manchester, 1997.

Serrão, V. 'A Pintura Maneirista em Portugal', in *História da Arte Portuguesa* (ed. P. Pereira) 3 vols; vol 2, pp. 429 ff.

1755: Catástrofe, Memória e Arte (ed. H.C. Buescu). Lisbon, 2006.

Silva, J.C. da, and Luckhurst, G. *Sintra: A Landscape with Villas*. Lisbon, 1989.

Sitwell, S. *Portugal and Madeira*. London, 1954.

Smith, R.C. *The Art of Portugal: 1500–1800*. London, 1968.

Southey, R. *Letters Written during a Short Residence in Spain and Portugal*. London, 1797.

Tabucchi, A. *Declares Pereira*. London, 1995.

———. *The Missing Head of Damasceno Monteiro*. London, 1980.

Tavares, J.F. *Damião de Góis*. Lisbon, 1999.

The Lisbon Earthquake of 1755. Representations and Reactions (ed. T.E.D. Braun and J.B. Radnor). Oxford, 2005.

Terra da Moura Encantada. Museu sem Fronteiras, Lisbon 1999.

Vale, T.L.M. *O Beau Séjour: Uma Quinta Romântica de Lisboa*. Lisbon, 1992.

Vicente, G. *Obras Completas* (ed. M. Braga), vol. 4. Lisbon, 1971.

Virgil: *The Aeneid, the Georgics, the Eclogues* (trans. J.A. Rhoades). Oxford, 1957.

Voltaire (F-.M. Arouet). *Romans et Contes* (ed. de H. Bénac). Paris, 1960.

Watson, W.C. *Portuguese Architecture*. London, 1908.

Wilcken, P. *Empire Adrift*. London, 2005.

Wordsworth, W. *Poetical Works*. Oxford, 1966.

Zimler, R. *The Last Kabbalist of Lisbon*. London, 1998.

Index

Individual cafés, churches, cinemas, districts, squares and streets are entered collectively under the generic entries 'cafés', 'churches', 'districts', 'squares', and 'streets' respectively.